YOUTH
AND
TRUTH

YOUTH
AND
TRUTH

UNPLUG WITH SADHGURU

HarperCollins *Publishers* India

First published in India by HarperCollins Publishers 2022
4th Floor, Tower A, Building No. 10, Phase II, DLF Cyber City,
Gurugram, Haryana –122002
www.harpercollins.co.in

2 4 6 8 10 9 7 5 3 1

P-ISBN: 978-93-5489-540-1
E-ISBN: 978-93-5489-556-2

Cover design: Isha Foundation

Typeset in 11/14.8 Adobe Garamond Pro at
Manipal Technologies Limited, Manipal

Printed and bound at
Thomson Press (India) Ltd

𝟏 𝐢𝐧 🅞 🅨 HarperCollinsIn

CONTENTS

FOREWORD

THOSE WHO LIVE AND WORK closely with Sadhguru are no strangers to his unpredictable and unconventional ways. Yet, sometimes, his chameleon-like ability to adapt to situations and his visionary ability to alter situations are astonishing to witness. To be fair, before the *Youth and Truth* movement, Sadhguru gave us volunteers at the Isha Yoga Center a heads-up – that we would be seeing him in a very different avatar. We also had to rejig ourselves to be in sync with this avatar and the youth he was reaching out to.

Sadhguru began undergoing visible changes. He was riding his motorcycle more, and wearing a T-shirt and denims. His choice of words and style of communication were becoming more informal and wittier than usual. Despite his white beard, he seemed to embody a youth. In fact, he exemplified what he had said before: that "youth" need not necessarily be linked with age, that youthfulness is very much in one's outlook – in not jumping to conclusions but willing to look at life fresh all the time. This movement was as much for the "youthful" as it was for the "youth".

To gear up and breathe life into this new movement, the various departments at Isha Foundation had to undergo a dramatic transformation and exhibit their youthfulness. It was as if our daily Yogic practices, which involved bending and twisting the body, found a new arena – summoning a new flexibility on the mental scape! The Sounds of Isha, accustomed to producing profound devotional songs, found themselves dabbling in the genre of rap music and strumming the electric guitar. The website team wracked their brains on how to create a "cool" *Youth and Truth* site. The media team had to move beyond the realm of TV and newspaper and enlist young YouTube stars and Instagram sensations to engage with Sadhguru. The design team shed the elegant motifs used for Isha's brochures and began doodling in earnest to make graffiti art.

It was in August 2018, at the end of a long conference call, that Sadhguru told the Isha core team, "Get ready." What followed was a whirlwind month of *Youth and Truth* events at colleges and universities across India. Sadhguru was adamant that these be interactive sessions with students, not a monologue by him. It was to be a "gossip", as captured by the byline of the movement: *Exploring truth not with the seriousness of gospel but with the playfulness of gossip.* He wanted students to ask him *whatever* they wanted, not inhibited by pressure or influence from teachers or parents. Nothing was off limits – from topics that were taboo, politically incorrect or controversial, to matters that were very personal, vulnerable and honest. They were even free to question Sadhguru himself and all that he stands for!

And so, in the run-up to the first event, Isha volunteers went all out to let the millennial generation know what was in store for them. Youth saw advertisements of a Ducati-riding Guru, watched their film idols interviewing him, and heard the audacious, grilling questions in the "*Poochu Kya?*" rap songs on social media. Sadhguru's tweet only added to the momentum: "Social media is gossip gone global. Let's raise it to the next level. When you gossip with a Mystic, your gossip goes cosmic."

Gradually, "Youth and Truth – Unplug with Sadhguru" started buzzing in student groups, generating excitement. But still, students had reservations about what to ask a Guru. Isha volunteers struggled to convince them that Sadhguru was open to taking any kind of question from them. It was only after the video of the first event went viral online that students could fathom how lively and approachable Sadhguru was. They happily let down their guard and brought out their deepest questions. The festive atmosphere at the events also helped everyone to loosen up. Concerts by pop singers had everyone dancing, and martial arts performances by Isha Samskriti students left one and all in awe. Sadhguru mingled with the youthful audience, taking selfies, or going to play a round of frisbee or football with them. They discovered in Sadhguru someone they could "unplug" with – who did not conform to established sets of tradition or ideology, who was unprejudiced, all-inclusive.

This book is an attempt to provide a glimpse into some of the most insightful conversations from the series of *Youth and Truth* events of September 2018, as well as later events that took place in India and abroad. It features the full talks at: Shri Ram College of Commerce, New Delhi; Regional Institute of Education, Demonstration Multipurpose School, Mysuru (Sadhguru's alma mater); Indian Institute of Technology, Bombay; Banaras Hindu University, Varanasi; and Columbia Business School, New York. Following each talk is a candid, behind-the-scenes account from students and volunteers.

Youth and Truth demonstrated the power of a question. We hope readers can recognize and celebrate this power in their lives. Questions that have the power to tear down assumptions and allow new perspectives to dawn, to shake societal structures and pave the way for change, to kindle more questions and lead us towards the wonder of discovery, and to nurture empathy, acceptance and bring us together as one.

Isha Publications

INTRODUCTION

IN THE LAST THIRTY-FIVE YEARS that I've been active with people, there has been a constant refrain: thousands of people ask me, "Sadhguru, where were you when I was twenty? You have come when I am sixty. If you had come when I was twenty, I would have lived differently – I would have done this, I would have done that." I've been hearing this continuously, so I decided to step out and meet all those people who are below twenty-five. That's how this *Youth and Truth* came about.

What we call as life is essentially a combination of a certain amount of time and energy. Time is passing for all of us at the same pace. If we sit, it passes. If we stand, it passes. If we do something, it passes. If we laze around, it will pass. Awake or asleep, time is rolling for all of us. Time is not manageable; the only thing we can really manage is our energies.

When you are in that segment of life which is known as youth, you are at the peak of your energy. This is something most youth do not realize till it passes. Life is not going to be the same as the years roll. When this energy – which is the only manageable part of our life – is raging at its peak, if we can bring ourselves to a certain level of clarity and balance, it could become a phenomenal force in our life. This energy could become a possibility to unfold our genius.

Every individual has a certain genius within them. Will they find the necessary atmosphere, attitude, and situation within and around themselves to unfold this? That is the only question. Unfortunately, I think not even one percent of the human population manages to really let their genius blossom in their life because they are too concerned with their livelihood. Very few people remain unconcerned and explore the possibility of what can be done at their peak.

My endeavor is to raise this percentage to ten percent in this generation. Then we will have a brilliant and phenomenal world, because, after all, a society, nation and the world are the products of human genius. Whether we live as a mediocre society or exceptional society is not decided by the masses on the street, but those few brilliant minds which shine in each generation. If we increase the percentage of that brilliance and allow it to unfold in a society, that society will flourish in a different way. Individual genius has always been the focus in Indian culture, because ultimately *that* is the determining factor. That is why, as part of *Youth and Truth*, I have been frequenting universities, to assist the youth in this process of igniting their genius.

"Youth are natural seekers of truth. Time to empower them with the needed clarity, commitment, and courage to find their truth."

SHRI RAM COLLEGE OF COMMERCE, NEW DELHI

4 September 2018

Sadhguru: Namaskaram and good morning to everyone. So this endeavor called *Youth and Truth* is going to last for some time. And it's our privilege – and your privilege – that SRCC is the first institution where we are starting. [*Applause*]

Shriram (Moderator): Namaskaram, Sadhguru. There is no need of much elaboration as to how privileged we are to have you amongst us.

Sadhguru: You can introduce yourself.

Shriram: So, I'm Shriram.

Sadhguru: You were born here? [*Laughs*]

Shriram: [*Laughs*] It so happens. I'm a third-year BCom Honors student.

Pranit (Moderator): Namaskaram, Sadhguru. I'm Pranit from Ludhiana and I'm a second-year BCom student.

Riya (Moderator): Namaskaram, Sadhguru. I'm Riya. I'm a first-year BA Economics Honors student.

Shriram: We all are fortunate to have gotten this opportunity to mediate this event.

Sadhguru: No. Mediation comes in only when we have a fight. [*Shriram laughs*] We don't have a fight, so…

Shriram: A lot of people had a lot of questions to ask, and we have tried our best to shortlist them and put forward whatever is relevant. Sadhguru, all of us sitting in this hall have some goals. And as most of us are students, our goals are at the maximum level. We are very eager to know, when you were our age, what was that thing which you wanted to become? What was your goal?

Sadhguru: Oh, this is beginning like an interrogation! [*Laughter*] Well, frankly I had no goal of any kind, to such a point that my father used to say, "What will this boy do? He's not interested in anything." Well, it was completely wrong. I was not interested in the things that *he* was interested in, but I was absolutely interested in many, many things.

See, when we say "goals", we must understand this – if you set a goal for your life from where you are, you can only set a goal according to your present level of understanding and knowledge, isn't it? You think you've reached a point where you know everything in the universe? So if you set a goal, what kind of goal will you set? A very meager goal. And if you grow rapidly, you will be terribly disappointed with your own goal.

But this has been taught to you in the recent years that you must be goal-oriented.

Let's say you want mangoes in your house – you don't have to think of mangoes. You have to think of soil, manure, water, sunlight. None of them look or taste like mangoes. But if you take care of those things, mangoes will come. Suppose you have a strong desire for mangoes, but you did nothing about growing a mango tree in your home; you will want to steal them from him [*pointing to Pranit*] if he has them. Yes or no?

Every year, we have a business event in the month of November. All the top business leaders have been there. Two hundred CEOs come every year to train with us for four days. So last year, one of them, who is running a major multinational company, was asking me, "Sadhguru, we pick the best from the IITs and the IIMs, and we keep paying them more and more, and they keep asking for more and more. But when I look at your organization, you pay nothing to any of them, and it seems to function many times better than our corporation. What is the secret?"

I said, "See, this is all it is – we are devoted to the process; we are not concerned about the goal." We are absolutely devoted to the process. Because if you do not do what you're doing right now well, your goal is just going to be a fancy desire, isn't it?

Audience: Yes.

Sadhguru: I would tell the young people, "Don't set a goal." If you have absolute devotion to what you're doing right now, depending upon the times and the opportunities, you will go as far as you go. But if you're always concerned about the finish line and not the step that you're taking right now, you will most probably fall flat on your face. If you get to the goal, you will be disappointed. If you don't get there, you will be broken.

I want you to look at it. Don't just go by what I say. Just go on the street and watch people. Leave the people who are driving a bullock cart and this and that. Watch those people who are driving BMWs, Mercedes and whatever else. Carefully watch the successful people. How many of them are joyfully driving their BMW or their dream car that they worked for? You will see hardly anybody, unless it's a stolen car! [*Laughter*]

So those who have gotten to their goals are disappointed, and those who could not get there are broken and frustrated. What's the point of a life like this?

Your ability to do things is enhanced only when you're absolutely devoted to the process you're involved in. I'm using the word "devotion" intentionally, because people think devotion means going to the temple. You tell me, in any arena of life – sport, art, music, politics, spirituality, academics, name it whatever you want – has anybody reached any significant levels of achievement without being devoted to what they're doing? Hello?

Audience: No.

Sadhguru: They have done mediocre things. But only those who are absolutely devoted to what they're doing have done significant things on this planet, and that's what you must do. [*Applause*]

Pranit: Sadhguru, so as you told us, those who achieve their goals aren't that happy…

Sadhguru: [*Makes a growling sound and pouncing motion, with fingers spread like claws; Pranit pauses*] I thought I'll just scare you a little bit. [*Laughter*]

Pranit: ...and those who don't have goals are also not happy, but goals are the starting point.

Sadhguru: No, no, no. Please let me correct this. Is a goal a starting point or a finishing line? Which is it?

Pranit: It's both ways. [*Laughs*]

Sadhguru: How is that? How is a goal a starting point? Please, you must tell me. All of you, is goal a starting point or a finishing line?

Audience: Finishing line.

Pranit: But goal is something that motivates us... like once we think of a goal in mind...

Sadhguru: Ah, you're coming to the point now. So, you have been trained like a circus monkey. [*Laughter*] You know, circus monkeys are like this – if you want them to do a trick, you have to give them a sweet. [*Gestures like a circus monkey; audience laughs*] Otherwise, "I won't do it." Then, one more little sweet. Don't be a circus monkey. I thought we evolved out of being monkeys a long time ago.

You're only working because of "What will I get? What will I get?" What the hell will you get? You'll die one day, that's all. [*Applause*] You think you're going to get something in the end? No, you're just going to die one day. The question is only how beautiful, significant and intense a life you have lived. That's all there is. Goal is an end point, isn't it? What do you think you'll get at the end of your life? I want you to visit old age homes and hospices where people are reaching the end of their lives. Just look at them. What do you think they have got? Nothing. Either they lived a profound life or they did not. That's all there is.

Pranit: Sadhguru, humans, and especially youngsters, have a lot of desires in their lives. But many a time we all are told, "Be content with what you have." But it comes to my mind that if we're satisfied, won't that lead to an end to progress?

Sadhguru: I don't know what kind of teachers you have met who told you, "Be content." Well, the word "contentment" comes from the word meaning containment. If you think containing your life is an answer, this is simply because you're just shit scared of life. That's all it is. See, if you step out into the world, something may happen to you. Possible? [*No response from audience*] Hey, are we on talking terms or no? What's the problem here?

Audience: Yes!

Sadhguru: If you step out of the house, something may happen.

Audience: Yes.

Sadhguru: Anything may happen – life may happen, death may happen, injury may happen, terrible things may happen, wonderful things may happen. Yes or no?

Audience: Yes.

Sadhguru: So one day, something a little terrible happened to you. Now, you come to your philosophy: "Don't step out of your house. Something terrible may happen to you." Yes, it may happen. But something absolutely wonderful can also happen to you. If you contain yourself, you can avoid both. Essentially, you're trying to insulate yourself against life. People come to me and say, "Sadhguru, please bless us that nothing should happen to us."

I say, "What kind of blessing is this? My blessing is, let everything happen to you! Let everything that's life happen to you." [*Applause*] First thing you must decide is, have you come here to avoid life or have you come here to experience life? Please make up your mind right now.

Audience: Experience!

Sadhguru: Well, if you want to experience your life, it doesn't mean you must get intoxicated. If you want to experience your life, that doesn't mean every evening you have to party. If you want to experience your life, you must bring this one instrument that you have to experience life [*referring to the human system*] to its highest possible sensitivity. If this becomes supersensitive, it will experience everything in the universe. If you keep it dull and lethargic, you will be right here; you won't know what the hell is happening around you.

Right now, because people are heavily goal-oriented, they don't know what's happening around them. They are only interested in the finishing line. The finishing line comes as a consequence of a certain efficient process. It does not come because you desire it. Success does not come because you desire it. It will not happen to those who are just desiring it; it will only happen to those who are doing the right things right now. [*Applause*]

Riya: So Sadhguru, you have always emphasized on how important clarity is in comparison to confidence or courage. But for people of our generation, confidence is something that's at a different level. Even when my nerves were racking to be here on the stage with you...

Sadhguru: Really?

Riya: Yes. [*Laughs*]

Sadhguru: Do I look so dangerous?

Riya: No.

Sadhguru: [*Laughs*] No, you're safe, don't worry. I was only trying to scare him [*pointing to Pranit*], not you. [*Laughter*]

Riya: Each of my friends emphasize on how confident I should be. So, do you think that overrating confidence has led to undermining the importance of clarity?

Sadhguru: Very much. See, confidence means this: now this hall is reasonably well lit. If I ask you to walk from there to there, do you need confidence?

Riya: No.

Sadhguru: Why? Because you can see things clearly. If we turn off the lights, make it pitch dark, and I ask you to walk from there to there, do you need confidence?

Riya: No.

Sadhguru: You do. If I ask you to walk in total darkness on the street, don't you need confidence?

Riya: Yeah.

Sadhguru: Why? No clarity. So, somebody thought confidence is a substitute for clarity. Let's say, you can't see clearly. You want to cross one of the main streets in Delhi. How to build confidence? Well, you can say "Jai Shri Ram" and run across the street. Or you can say "Allah-hu-Akbar" or "Hail Mary" and run across the street. You may make it just by sheer chance or because of the compassion of some driver. [*Laughter*] But if you try this every day, we know where to pick you up. [*Applause*]

I'm asking, is confidence really a substitute for clarity? The problem is like this... You take a coin and flip it: "Heads – 'I will do it.' Tails – 'I will not do it.'" There are a whole lot of people in the world who are doing this. The problem with the coin is that it has only two faces; the problem with life is that it has a million faces. So, this heads and tails looks like it solves your problem, but for those who are right only fifty percent of the time in their lives, there are only two professions left. They can either become a weather person and predict weather, or an astrologer. In any other profession, they'll be fired. [*Applause*]

See, it happens many times that if you just run across the street, you make it. That's the whole problem. There is an element of chance in life through which you can make it. This is something young people must decide, it is very important: Do you want to build your life on chance or on your competence?

Audience: Competence!

Sadhguru: Suppose you're successful by chance, you're always insecure and fearful, isn't it?

Audience: Yes.

Sadhguru: If you've made it by your competence, then it's a different matter – if this doesn't work, we'll do something else; if that doesn't work, we'll do something else. Because we built a competence. But if you're living by chance, then if you make it, you're fearful you'll lose the position. If you don't make it, of course, you know the pain. [*Applause*]

Pranit: So Sadhguru, nowadays we see a lot of young people are in relationships. A public display of affection (PDA) is quite common and popular among the young generation, and it's very normal for all of us to, you know, hug our friends or kiss our partners openly in front of others. But our previous generation consider PDA as something vulgar. It's very strange that love offends someone. So, my question is, whose outlook do you support? That of the young generation or of your own generation? [*Laughter*]

Sadhguru: What makes you think you're younger than me? [*Cheers*] No, no, I don't agree that you're younger than me! [*Laughs*]

There are many aspects to this question. You said that today young people have relationships. Unfortunately, you have come to a place where you think that a relationship means it must be body-based, that there must be something biological involved. Biology is a part of our life. But the significance of becoming human compared to other creatures is they're complete biology and we are only part biology. We have other dimensions to us. We have an intelligence. We have an emotion. We have a consciousness which is of another dimension. Biology is only one part of us.

If an earthworm says, "I have a relationship," and two of them tangle each other, I understand. If a human being says, "I have a relationship," it could be a friend, a brother, a sister. It could be a variety of relationships and also body-based relationships. So, using the word "relationship" only with biological stuff is essentially because somewhere, unknowingly, may be because of the internet, you've gotten enslaved to America. It all started in the United States. Relationship means it has to be about the opposite sex, or something sexual. Why can't you hold relationships of other kinds? Are we not capable? Can't we have every kind of intimate, profound relationship with people without fondling their bodies? I'm asking, possible or no?

Audience: Yes.

Sadhguru: Biology is not the most prominent aspect of being human. It is there. It's not something you can put under the carpet. It is very much there, but it is not the dominant aspect of being human. With other creatures, it is so. With a human being, the most significant aspects are our intelligence, our emotion, our consciousness – these are big things. Body is just one part of it. I'm not saying you must ignore the body. Body is there.

Now when you say "young people", you're talking about those people whose intelligence has been hijacked by hormones. [*Laughter*] When you were ten years of age, you looked at people and everybody was fine. They were quite okay. You became fourteen, fifteen, and you looked at them – every little bump on their body suddenly became a world by itself. [*Laughter*] You have to wait for some more time. When the hormonal thing goes down, then you look at people, again they will all look normal. [*Applause*] So, it's not a question of right and wrong, it's not a question of morality. It is just a question of priority – what kind of priority you want to give to your own bodily compulsions.

Just now when I was coming to your college, somebody in a main street was standing there and urinating. When he feels like it, he does it. What's the problem? No problem! Because when you feel like it, you do whatever you want and you think it's your right. He also thinks it's his right – when he feels like it, he urinates on the street. "What's wrong? Dogs are doing it, donkeys are doing it, cattle are doing it. Everybody is doing it." [*Laughter*] "Be natural" – this is the philosophy you are talking about.

I'm saying, there is a certain sanctity to relationships, especially body-based relationships. If you don't maintain that sanctity, after some time it'll definitely become vulgarity. So, somebody is able to see it before you can, that if you go like this, tomorrow it'll lead to something else. This does not mean being a moral prude. No. But if you don't maintain that sanctity, you will regret how relationships will become. Later on, you will see how much pain they can bring in your life.

So, you're talking about the previous generation. I neither belong to that nor do I belong to your generation. I belong to the future generations, that's why I'm like this! [*Laughs*] [*Applause*] The previous generation that you're talking about was a generation which came just post-Independence. You must understand their reality. They lived as an occupied nation for a period of time. Some of them fought, others slinked around. Whichever way, their ideas of morality, essentially, were of their masters. It is British prudery that they carried within themselves. Their idea of being "right" is that they must be in a straitjacket all the time. You don't have to go by that, neither do you have to do something stupid in reaction to that. You must conduct your life sensibly. You must conduct your life in such a way that this will work for you for your entire life, in some sense.

You do something wacky today, and there may be a payment tomorrow. So, why don't you think it through – what is the best thing to do? How much of what should I do? How much of body, how much of intelligence, how much of emotion, how much of consciousness. In your life, you must decide which should dominate your life. Accordingly, you conduct it – it's fine. Somebody doesn't like it, they need not see it. [*Applause*]

Shriram: Sadhguru, now I want to ask you something out of the context. So, when we all sat for deciding on the questions which we want to ask, a girl came up with something very unique which she noticed in you, and we felt it is relevant. Why is it that wherever you go to kind of preach or talk about stuff, you sit in a particular position? You know, with the sandal removed from your left foot, left leg up and your right leg on the ground intact. Is it your style or is it a way that one should sit?

Sadhguru: Do you still use the Indian toilet? [*Laughter*]

Shriram: Yeah.

Sadhguru: Yes. Do you sit in a particular way? [*Applause*] I am just asking you, do you? Why? Because the body is made like that. I forget the name of the university – some university in the United States did a study and they said, "This is the best way to shit!" [*Laughter*] Because your thighs will go into your abdomen and press it out. Everything that needs to come out will come out. If what needs to come out doesn't come out, it will slowly rise to your head. [*Laughter*] Yes!

So, in the Yogic sciences we observed that certain types of body positions will support one to perform different types of activity to the best. Or, in other words, in what is called as Hatha Yoga, the physical postures are about manipulating the body in such a way that you get to a certain geometric perfection, that your geometry is aligned with the larger geometry of creation so that you are always in sync, you are never off. And how balanced you are, how clearly you see things and how well you do things, simply depend on how much you are in sync with everything else around you. Whether it's people or trees or life or just space, whether you are in sync with it or not will decide how smooth, how friction-free your function is in the world. Now, I don't sit like this all the time – only when I speak.

If I have to explain how I am sitting… There is something called as Siddhasana. There are many aspects to it. One simple aspect is, there is a point on the left heel that today the medical sciences are calling the "Achilles". You've heard of that? You've heard of the man, Achilles? [*Talking to Pranit*] You didn't see the movie *Troy*? [*Pranit shakes his head*] An innocent boy! So, you put your Achilles at what is called the *muladhara* or the perineum in your body. If these two things touch, many aspects are cleared out within you for that period of time. Your thoughts are clear, your emotions are calmed, and there is a very clear perception of what's happening around you.

You've heard that Achilles was killed because an arrow was shot to his heel. You don't believe if somebody hurts your heel, you will die. Isn't it so? But Achilles died that way. And there is another person who died that way in India, way before him.

Audience: Krishna.

Sadhguru: Yesterday was his birthday – Krishna Janmashtami. He also died in this way. What this is trying to tell you is that they were killed in an expert way. Not just slitting your throat or breaking your head, but just putting a point at the Achilles – so they had to die.

There is a certain energy system in the body. If that point of Achilles is in touch with your muladhara, when you sit like this, there is a certain balance, that you don't take any sides. See, all of us have our own opinions, ideas, ideologies, stuff – our own experiences of life. Your own experiences of life and imprints that you have taken in your mind influence everything that you see. You like this person, you don't like this person, you love that person, you hate this person – all this is because you are constantly taking positions of your own. But if you really want to know life, the most important thing is you don't take any position. You're willing to look at everything absolutely fresh every moment of your life.

This is very difficult for people to understand. People who have been with me every day for thirty, thirty-five years, working with me, doing so many things – I still don't have a single opinion about them. Only when I need to do some work, I may look at their competence and stuff. But I don't have a single opinion about anybody who is around me for such a long time. By now you should have formed your opinions, but I don't, because that is the essence of the spiritual process – that we're constantly looking at every life as a possibility.

There is, of course, a distance between possibility and reality. Some will have the courage and commitment to travel that distance. Some will not. But every life is a possibility. If you want to keep that possibility open, you never ever form an opinion of any sort about anybody. Good, bad, ugly – you don't form these opinions. You simply look at them right now. How are they right now, this moment – that's all that matters to me. How you were yesterday is not my business. How you may be tomorrow, let's see. Tomorrow must be created, not concretized right now, isn't it? [*Applause*]

It's a certain geometry of the body. I'm telling you, right now, the Western cultures are going about propagating, "Yoga is another stretching exercise. Instead of that, you can do Pilates, you can do boxing, you can play tennis." See, if you want to be just fit, then go run somewhere, climb a mountain, play tennis, do something. Yoga is not about fitness. Fitness is just one consequence.

The important thing is to get the right geometry of life, because the physical universe is all geometry. Now, this building is standing here. How long will it stand? Whether it will fall on our head today or stand for a long time essentially depends on how geometrically perfect it is. The same goes for the body, the same goes for the planetary system, the same goes for the universe, the same goes for everything. Planet Earth is not going around the sun with a steel cable attached to it. Just perfection of geometry, isn't it? If a little off-geometry happens, it's gone forever – and that's true with you also. If you go off your fundamental geometry, you are gone.

It's very important that at an early age you do the right things to bring a right sense of geometry – now, you become competent to go through life. Those people who are thinking only good things should happen to them, obviously, they are unfit for life. Because, if you do not know how to go through harsh situations well, joyfully, then you will avoid all possibilities, isn't it? You will avoid all great possibilities of life, simply because you want to avoid a little bit of difficulty. Only when you are geometrically in a certain state of congruence, are you willing to go through any situation no matter what it is. [*Applause*]

Riya: That was really profound.

Sadhguru: *Achcha?*

Riya: Sadhguru, jealousy is always considered as a really cynical emotion. But to be honest, for me, it has worked so well…

Sadhguru: [*Laughs*] What did you get to do, hm?

Riya: It motivates me. [*Sadhguru laughs*] So, every time my friend learns something new, I just get this innate urge to perform better. And it's probably why I have landed up in my dream college. So, do you think that jealousy is actually a negative emotion, or does it motivate you to do better?

Sadhguru: See, these days fortunately it's gone. When we were growing up, especially when Diwali came, in small towns, one fun that people had was to fill a can with firecrackers and tie it to a donkey's tail. When it went *dum dum dum!*, the poor donkey ran all over the place faster than a horse. You think that's the way to motivate life? [*Applause*] There are better and more intelligent ways of doing things. Well, when you feel like your tail is burning, you may run. If a dog is chasing you, you will run really fast. But, you know Mr Bolt? He does not run because his tail is on fire. He runs because he has prepared his legs and lungs in such a way, whichever way he runs, he is faster than everybody. Isn't that the way to run? [*Applause*]

You want to run either because a dog is chasing you or because your tail is on fire. No, that's not a pleasant way to run. One thing is, it is important that you run fast. Another thing is that your experience of running is fantastic. Isn't that important?

Audience: Yes.

Sadhguru: Well, you got into your dream college, but it could be three years of hell, who knows? Is it not important that these three years are a fantastic experience for you? Running is not the only important thing. Suppose we ran because our tails were on fire – now we understand the only way to make people run is to set their tails on fire. How much damage we will cause to everybody! And, I've seen these donkeys running faster than a race horse because they're terrified. That's not the way to run. Please don't do that to yourself. Not anymore, okay? Now the dream has come true. [*Applause*]

Riya: Yeah.

Shriram: Sadhguru, now that we talked about her dream college...

Sadhguru: Hey, it's okay. You were born here, so it's all right. [*Laughter*]

Shriram: ...I take the leverage of putting you in a situation. Suppose you are a third-year student at SRCC. Most of the third-years would join me in the mindset that this is the time, you know, where we have a lot of options – we can opt for placements, we can do higher studies, we can pursue CA, etc. But at times it so happens that our mission or our goal about life is different from that of our parents. Have you ever come across such a situation where your goals are not in line with your parents', and is it okay to kind of go against them?

Sadhguru: See, they had goals and goals. I had none. So I never came across such a thing. [*Applause*] My father is a very good man, and academically, all his life he's been at the top, and he's a physician. In India, we have a malice that, first thing is you become a doctor. If you cannot, you become an engineer. If you cannot, then only you end up in commerce. [*Laughter*] At least in the previous generation. When we were growing up, that was the thing. So obviously, his dream was I should become a doctor. I hope he is not on the web, listening to me! Because he studied in such a way that for him it was a passion. He lost his mother when he was four years of age – she died of tuberculosis. So, though he is from a very large business family, he committed that he will become a doctor. Because somewhere, a four-year-old boy felt that if there was a good doctor, his mother would have lived. For him, being a doctor was not a profession; it was like his religion. He lived like that. So naturally, he wanted all his four children to become doctors. First one didn't become a doctor, second one didn't, third one didn't, and I got caught. [*Laughter*]

At the age of ten or eleven, I clearly told him, "See, one thing is I'm never going to be a doctor. Please don't pin your hopes on me."

He showed me all his piles of notes that he'd kept during his studies. He said, "I've kept all this so that one of you will become a doctor." Well, all three went different ways, and me going nowhere. [*Laughter*] I am only interested in biology, which means I'm interested in the jungle – not in dissecting something, but just in looking and absorbing things.

So a time came when I finished my – what do you call Plus Two today?

Riya: Twelfth grade.

Sadhguru: Twelfth. At that time, it was called "pre-university course". I finished my twelfth standard and I decided I will not go to the university. By then I had cycled across southern India, I had seen more life than most people would have seen. I had done some small trading of this and that, and earned a lot of money. "Lot" means in those days a few thousand rupees. Maybe I had 50,000 to 60,000 rupees when I was seventeen years of age. All rolled up. I didn't know what's banking, so I rolled it up and put rubber bands, and hid it all over so that my brother doesn't steal it.

I had a lot of money, and I had a bicycle, and I wanted to go to Moscow on my bicycle. I was preparing for that. So, I was not going to the university, for sure. In this family, if you fail, there's an advantage – you don't go to the university. If I knew that, I would've just failed. But the problem is I'd passed. So I said, "I won't go to the university. I will educate myself."

He said, "What? Not going to the university?"

I said, "No."

Then, once I said I'm not going to the university, suddenly, I became such an evil in the family. Everybody started looking at me like, "What is wrong with you?" I couldn't understand. What are they reacting to? I don't want to go to the university, what is their problem? First of all, I never understood why I should go to the university.

That one whole year, just to handle the reaction I got, I did something very unique and uncharacteristic of me. I went to the Mysore University library every day. When the library opened at nine o'clock, I was there. I was the first customer. When it closed at eight o'clock, I was the last one to get out. These days, many of you are well-fed – those days we were also well-fed, but the level of activity was such, I was always hungry. At that time, I would actually eat at least ten times more than what I eat today. So, no matter how much I ate, I was always hungry. But this one year, I went without a lunch. It's not a small thing. You [*pointing at Pranit*] can easily go without lunch. But for me, who was scrawny and had a concave stomach all the time, going without lunch for one year was like a big feat.

I just read anything to anything. You know, from Kalidasa to Homer, to popular mechanics, to many, many years of National Geographic, and all kinds of books on physics, mathematics, astronomy, whatever. One whole year, every day, eleven hours a day, I read and read and read. That's the only reading I did. After that, me and books don't go together.

Then, after one year, I realized that just gathering all this information is a waste of time for me. And when the next academic year came, there was drama at home. My mother was crying and said, "What are you wasting your life for? We thought you will become this, you will become that."

I said, "I don't know what I'll become."

But she put so much pressure: "Just get into some college. Whether you go there or not, I will not ask. Just get into some college."

Then I thought through this and I said, "Okay, I'll do English literature." Because in this one year, I had developed some appetite for reading literature and poetry, and I myself was writing many poems about just anything. So I joined literature. I went to college.

First day, a teacher came and read a book. Everybody was writing down *karrah karrah*.* These days it doesn't make noise, but those days, the fountain pens – fifty people were writing *karrah karrah*. I didn't like this. I just looked into the teacher's book. Then I saw it is a handwritten book, her notes. I said, "Ma'am, if you give that book to me, I'll make photocopies of this and give it to everybody. You don't have to come, we don't have to come." [*Applause*] "But if you want me to come here, I have millions of questions – like a dark cloud, it's hanging around my head. I'm going to ask these questions. If you cannot answer these questions, I cannot sit here." Then, I made a deal with all the teachers that they give me attendance, and I won't bother them with questions. [*Applause*] This deal worked pretty well for three years and I got out.

Is this what my father wanted? Definitely not. I'm saying this to you not so that you simply go against your parents – that's not the point. The point is, this life is precious. Now when you're talking about "What shall I do? Shall I do this, shall I do that?" – is it only about how to earn a living? You must get off that. Education is not about earning a living. When an earthworm,

---

* Scratching sounds of pens.

grasshopper, every insect, bird and animal can earn a living, what is the big deal about survival with such a big brain?

Survival is not the big thing for the human being. Survival has become a problem because you want to survive like somebody else. That's the whole problem. If you want to survive, it's not a problem. My father would ask, "How will you make a living? How will you live? What will you earn?"

I said, "If nobody wants to feed me, I'll go into the jungle." Many times, I went off into the forest and just survived off the forest without any food support from anywhere else.

So, survival is not the issue. What are we going to do with this life? Are we going to take this life to full potential, or are we going to be those people who are just shit scared of life itself? "What will happen to my food, what will happen to my food?" What is this? When a street dog is not bothered, happily wagging his tail and going about *tuk tuk tuk*, what is your problem with such a big brain? You don't educate for survival. You educate because you want to expand your horizons. You want to make this life into a worthwhile life. That's what matters. [*Applause*] Will it be in conflict with many people? Of course, it will be. Because they think you won't make it.

I must tell you this, now that you asked this question. This was almost thirty-four years ago. There was a person who was like a godfather to my wife at that time. She was still working in a bank. I was living on my motorcycle, traveling all over the place. I would teach here and there once in three to four months, but the rest of the time I was simply riding across the country with no purpose. So, one day I came to Bangalore, and I went to their home because the entire night I'd been riding. I wanted to shower and have some food, and then go pick up my wife from the bank. I showered and ate well. And then this man sat in front of me and said, "See, I know somebody in the Bangalore Development Authority. In this particular extension there are some house sites available. You must get yourself a house site."

I said, "What? Me, buy a house site? For what? I live on the motorcycle. Why will I buy a house site?"

He said, "No, you're married. You can't be like this. You need to have a house someday. You must buy a house site."

I said, "Don't you tell me this. If I want to buy real estate, I wouldn't buy a house site; I will buy a town. Okay? So, that's not my interest at all. I'm not going to buy a house site, please don't try to push me. Thank you for the meal and the shower, but…"

Then he looked at me hopelessly and asked, "How long will you go on like this?"

I said, "As long as my marbles roll." That's about it. That's how long everybody goes about in their life.

Then I went out. After eighteen years of no contact, he called me in 2017. Because the government gave me this Padma Vibhushan, he called me and he said, "I never thought your marbles will roll this far!" [Applause]

See, the problem is just this – people value something only because it's recognized by somebody. That means they're blind, isn't it? If you look at this light, you must know this is light. If you look at this and don't know what it is, and I say, "See, that is light," that means you're blind. Yes or no? Unfortunately, a whole lot of people can see light only when you say it is light; otherwise they can't see it. Don't go by such people, whoever they may be. It doesn't matter who they are. [Applause]

Pranit: So, Sadhguru…

Sadhguru: You can hold the mic close, it's not dangerous. [*Laughter*]

Pranit: Okay. So, expression of opinion is a fundamental right given to all the citizens of the country. And we youngsters, born in the era of social media, are not at all hesitant about expressing our opinions on social platforms or to anyone. But there are times when by expressing our opinion, we might hurt someone's sentiments, or other people might get offended by what we say. So in such a situation, how should a youngster use the tool of social media and express his opinion in a very balanced way so that no one is hurt?

Sadhguru: In 280 characters, some of the world leaders are expressing the policy of the nation, all right? They're even setting foreign policy agenda of major nations in 280 characters on Twitter. So I was telling these Twitter people, "You guys are missing something tremendous just for the numbers [of accounts]. Tomorrow the entire world may set its agenda and policy on Twitter. But that will not happen simply because for seven billion people you have fifteen billion accounts. Most of them are fake." People who don't have the courage to put their name out and say "This is what I want to say" are slinks; this is not opinion, isn't it?

Young people must do this: You can say what you want, but you must have the courage to stand up and say, "Okay, this is what I will say." Not hide under the chair and say something loudly. What is the point of such a life? What is the point of such an existence? Is it not important that whatever you say, you're accountable for it? Hello?

Audience: Yes!

Sadhguru: All of you who are managing fake Facebook
accounts, Twitter accounts, take them away and put your name
out there – "This is me and this is what I say. You like it, or
you don't like it. If you don't like it, please tell me. I will look
at it. If you don't like it, you explain to me why you don't like
it, then I will consider." But you don't even want to put your
name on it and you want to express your opinion all over the
world. No, you have no right to do such things just because you
have technological tools. Okay? I can't stand behind this board
[*pointing to the backdrop on the stage*] and shout something at
you. If I want to say something, I must be able to say it to you,
isn't it?

Without responsibility, you should not claim an authority
over everybody's life. I don't have authority over your life to say
whatever I want about your life and what you do. If I want to
say something, I must take some responsibility for that, isn't it?
If this is brought about, everybody can say what they want to say.

Only thing is, you're talking about if it hurts somebody. See,
let's understand this. Speech is communication. Communication
between who? Two people. Isn't it so? Two groups of people
or two individuals or whatever. When I'm speaking to you, is
it not important that whatever I wish to say I can say? Is it not
important that I respect your position? I'm willing to listen to
what you say, and then I will say strongly whatever I want to say.
I will say it very strongly. See, look at me! What I say, I will say
it very strongly. "I'm not even willing to listen to you" – that is
not at all acceptable. But right now, that is the instrument social
media has given to people that they can say what they want

and they don't have to listen to anybody. If you say something, they will abuse you. Abuse is also language, isn't it so? Shall I use it right now on you? [*Speaking to Pranit*] Do you want to be abused by anybody? [*Pranit shakes his head*] So if you don't want to be abused by anybody, you must understand, nobody else wants to be abused either. [*Applause*]

Shriram: Sadhguru, so you have built such a huge Adiyogi statue at your ashram, and whoever visits that place is in awe of that particular statue. So do you think nowadays, in the current scenario, things have to be done in a mass scale to get noticed?

Sadhguru: No, there's only one statue, how is it a mass?

Riya: It's huge…

Shriram: It is built in such huge form.

Sadhguru: The size?

Shriram: Yeah.

Sadhguru: See, what is big and small is according to people's perceptions. All the people in the Yoga Center say, "Sadhguru, we should have made it a little bigger. It's looking so small compared to the mountain behind." So what is small and big is always people's perception, but there is something called visual impact. Of all the five sensory organs that you have – of seeing, hearing, smelling, tasting and touching – if I tell you, "I'm going to take four of these away from you right now," which one would you like to keep? Just the nose or just the tongue? This is an option. Four you have to lose, one you can keep. Which one will you keep?

Shriram: Everything is important.

Sadhguru: Everything is important, but you're going to lose four. You must learn to exercise these options, because life is like that. It won't let you keep everything, something you have to lose. Which four will you want to lose and which one thing will you want to keep?

Shriram: Can you just tell the five?

Sadhguru: Either I'll take off your eyes, or your eardrums, or your tongue, or your sensation, or your nose. Which one thing do you want to keep? Tell me.

Audience: Eyes!

Sadhguru: Eyes, of course. Because of the five sensory impacts that you have upon you, visual impact is the largest right now. So in that sense, it is not about the size of the Adiyogi; it is about the geometry. To get the geometry perfect in a small size is extremely difficult. So, we needed a certain size to get the geometry easily in place. The geometry of Adiyogi is to exude certain specific qualities.

Is it true that if you go home today and your father is sitting in a certain way, just by looking at his posture, you would know whether he's angry, happy, unhappy, or disturbed?

Audience: Yes.

Sadhguru: So, we wanted the geometry of Adiyogi to exude three aspects – one is exuberance of life, another is stillness of life, another is intoxication. I worked for two and a half years to get this face right. Many, many faces were made. Then we decided we needed a certain size, and that size became over eighty feet. When it became over eighty feet, we thought the number also has to have some significance. So, we went for

112 feet, because when Adiyogi propounded the different ways in which a human being can attain to their highest possibility, he gave 112 ways. It could have been eighty-seven feet. But I thought, if we are going for eighty-seven, what is the problem? We'll get it to a number that he likes. So it became 112 feet. But we wouldn't have been able to achieve the geometry of what we wanted in less than eighty to ninety feet. That's why it's 112 feet.

Riya: So Sadhguru, you are so revered and you are so cherished. Do you ever get a superiority complex?

Sadhguru: Right now, yes [*deepens his voice; straightens and glares at Riya*]. [*Laughter*] See, the question is not about superiority complex, inferiority complex, poverty complex or wealthy complex. That you have a complex is a serious problem, isn't it? Whatever kind it is! What a complex means is you have assumed something about yourself and you have concretized that assumption in such a way that you make a bloody fool of yourself wherever you go. Do I look like I'm making a bloody fool of myself with you?

Riya: No.

Sadhguru: No. So no complex of any kind.

Riya: All right. But then our confidence fluctuates every day, so what do you have to say about that?

Sadhguru: Because I don't have any confidence about anything, I just have clarity, people think I have knowledge. No, my head is empty. That's why to make it look a little substantial, I have a turban. [*Laughter*] It's totally empty, always, but I have clarity. Clarity means what? You see things the way they are. Knowledge means what? You have fixed information about everything. If things have changed, you will not see it the way it is. That's as good as being blind. See, people think owls are blind. It's not true. Their vision is far more sensitive than yours, but because of sunlight they're blinded – because it's too much. What is the power of your glasses?

Riya: Around 3.4.

Sadhguru: Let's say we put it at ten! Now, if you look at these lights, you'll feel dazzled. That's what is happening to an owl in the day. When light goes down, he sees very clearly, not because he's blind, but because his eyes are supersensitive. So, it's important that you bring clarity to your life, not knowledge, because knowledge is conclusions that you gather. Knowledge is okay when you're trying to do something physical, material, in the world, but not with life.

Is it true what you thought was absolute at the age of twelve is not true today? Yes or no? Are you sure that whatever you think as "this is it" right now will be "this is it" in another three years' time?

Riya: Of course not.

Sadhguru: You know that. So, you know you're wrong. [*Laughs*] Yes or no?

Riya: Yes.

Sadhguru: You know anyway you're wrong, so why assert the wrong things? Well, right now we are wrong, at least let's manage with a little more consciousness. If you know you're wrong, you will walk carefully, isn't it? But if you think you're absolutely correct, then you will do stupid things and blunder around the world. If you know you are not seeing properly, will you walk carefully or not? Suppose we turn off all the lights suddenly, will you not become super alert and conscious as to how you walk? But when the lights are on, you're just going unconsciously, bumping into everybody. So, if you learn to walk every moment like there are no lights and you're looking at everything absolutely carefully, then what you see clearly, you go through it; when you don't see clearly, you hesitate. Some places you take a little bit of chance. But if you are just confident, you will blunder through life; we don't know where you will get in and what you will get trapped into.

Most people are trapped in their professions, their family situations and their social situations in such a way that they all become like this [*shows a dull, zombie-like face*]. Yes? Already I'm seeing, not just older people, even the youth have become like this. "What will happen to me at the end of my life? What will happen to me at the end of my life?" I already revealed the secret: you will die. "But Sadhguru, if this happens what to do, if that happens what to do?" All those things will happen. It's not that everything will happen in your life the way you like it. Things will happen in the way you don't like.

It once happened. Shankaran Pillai got fired from his job simply because he asked a question – "Smoking or non-smoking?" How can you get fired for asking such a simple question? Because what he was supposed to ask was, "Cremation or burial?" You're not getting it? [*Laughter*]

Many times what you do thinking "I'm right" may be irrelevant to the situation in which you exist. The most important aspect of your life is you are relevant. Not right – you're just relevant to the existing situation. "I'm right, I'm right, I'm right!" This is confidence. Nobody cares about you being right. All the idiots who think they are right, nobody wants to listen to them, nobody wants to be around them, isn't it? People who always think "I'm right, I'm right" – you want to be around them? No. The important thing is you are relevant to the situation in which you exist. If you have to bring relevance into your life, you must extinguish your confidence and bring clarity.

There are many systems to develop clarity. See, to develop your muscle, there are systems, isn't it? Similarly, to develop clarity, there are many systems. Unfortunately, our education system is dulling clarity in so many ways. Some of the research studies in the university show that if a child goes to kindergarten and goes through twenty years of education – I'm sorry, I'm saying this at an educational institution! – and comes out with a PhD, they are saying seventy percent of their intelligence is irrevocably destroyed. So you have a knowledgeable idiot. What do you do with this? Well, you can impress people by throwing information. But this whole game of impressing people, throwing information around, is all going to go, because that Google lady is better than any of these idiots. [*Applause*]

It's really amazing. Let's say I'm flying to the United States, Africa or somewhere. I just ask, "What is the morning temperature in Entebbe? I'm landing there." Without batting an eyelid, in two seconds, she tells me it's fourteen degrees Centigrade, by afternoon it'll be eighteen degrees Centigrade, by evening it'll be twelve degrees Centigrade. Who could ever say this? She may not be perfectly right, but she's almost there. So, people who are carrying a basket of information on their heads and feeling superior, I want you to understand this. Just a few generations ago, somebody who could read a book was seen as godlike because everybody else was illiterate. And people thrived simply because they could read the Gita or the Bible or something else. But once everybody could read, we are ignoring those people completely. Yes or no?

Audience: [*Few people respond*] Yes.

Sadhguru: Tsk. You are falling asleep, I think. Hey, this is not a commerce class! [*Laughter*] So, people who are carrying information and feeling superior will all be made into nothing in the next fifteen to twenty years' time. Once artificial intelligence comes all over the place, information will mean nothing because it will be available everywhere. By then you must be competent to do something beyond information. This is why I'm with you. [*Applause*]

Riya: All right. So now before we open the session for our audience to ask you questions, we have some really popular questions from various social media platforms.

Sadhguru: Whoa!

Pranit: So the people who could not join here, they've sent us the questions through various social media platforms, and the first question, I'll read it out – "Sadhguru, you mentioned that you can do fourteen different activities at a given moment. So, we all are very curious to know, how can we achieve such prowess over both body and mind?"

Sadhguru: Oh! Whoever said this? I didn't say anything like that. Anyway, do you have a liver?

Pranit: Yes, I do.

Sadhguru: Functioning?

Pranit: Yes. [*Laughs*]

Sadhguru: Do you know how many levels of activity it's doing right now? What the liver is doing is far more complex than what your brains are doing right now. Do you know this? A brainless liver, if it can do so many things, a brained Pranit, how many things? No, I was not only talking about activity per se. But yes, activity is also possible. See, you must understand this. Are you on a round planet?

Audience: Yes.

Sadhguru: Spinning?

Audience: Yes.

Sadhguru: Most people don't understand this unless, you know, they get sozzled out with something, or they get some ailment where there's either a few drops more or a few drops less between the ears – suddenly you see the planet is round. Do you know how complex an activity it is for a human being to walk at a certain latitude on a round planet which is spinning and which has magnetic forces working upon you all the time? It's an extremely complex process. You ask a child who is one year of age, he knows how complex it is. Have you seen? But the moment you learn to walk, you assume that it's nothing. You are sick of walking. You want to drive a car, you want to ride a motorcycle. But walking is such a complex process. Your knees and your brains and the fluids in your body – all of them are doing not fourteen, but a thousand different functions all the time.

Anyway, you're doing it. If only you could conduct these things consciously, you would be doing a thousand things. So, I was only talking about different channels of the mind, which you don't have to actually conduct; you just have to initiate them and leave – it will go on. For you to think about your neighborhood girl, do you have to initiate action every time? No! I'm saying, if she's pretty, once you look at her, it just goes on by itself, isn't it? Because you are drawn to it. If you are drawn to ten different things at the same time, the mind is capable of creating ten different channels and keeping them running.

Right now, I think there is one Jain monk, a sixteen- or seventeen-year-old boy. You've heard of him? He's in the newspapers.

Pranit: Yes, Sadhguru.

Sadhguru: How many things can he do? Ten things or fifteen things. Anyway, there are people in small towns in southern India who are called Shatavadhanis; that means they can do one hundred things at the same time. A complex mathematical problem, a sensation, a music, some *raga*, this, that, a hundred things at the same time, because that is how complex the human mind is. You can use this complexity to drive yourself crazy with unbridled thought and emotion. If you harness it though, it can do things that nobody has imagined possible. It can do things in a miraculous way. You can manifest things in a phenomenal way if the necessary training goes into you. See, if somebody is walking there, if you just look at how they are walking, can you not make out whether they are physically fit or not? You can see the body has been worked upon.

Similarly, whether the mind has been worked upon or not, whether your energies have been worked upon or not, are things that are visible. Most people may not see, but if you pay attention, you will see. The most sophisticated machine on this planet is this human mechanism. Isn't it so?

Audience: Yes.

Sadhguru: I'm asking you, have you read the user's manual?

Audience: No.

Sadhguru: No? When are you going to read it? On the last day? When I see this ridiculous stuff, people reading the Gita when they are dying, I say, "You are reading the user's manual on the last day. What's the point?" If you buy a phone, should you read the user's manual in the first three days or after three years when you want to get rid of the phone?

Audience: First three days…

Sadhguru: You must read it in the first three days. So, I'm not asking you to read a scripture. Well, this [*referring to the human system*] is a living scripture. Should you not become competent to read this scripture, understand what is the nature of this, the full potential of it, and explore it? Because this life is not about this or that – this life is about *this one* [*referring to oneself*]. Yes or no? There is no choice about this. It is just that you can enslave this life to something else and think it's about that. But actually, it's about this, isn't it so? Are you okay with this?

You think right now your life is about education – no! Your life is about this one. You want this one educated. You want this one to do well. You want this one to experience love. You want this one to experience pleasure. You want this one to do all this. All the other things are only attendant things; this one is the real thing, isn't it?

So, if this is the real thing, does this deserve some amount of attention? "Some amount of attention" does not mean standing in front of the mirror and attending to your skin endlessly. Should you not pay attention to every dimension of what this human being is made of, what makes this life tick and how? If you understand what makes it tick, you can make it roar. If you can make it roar, why fourteen things? You can do many more! [*Applause*]

Shriram: Sadhguru, I'll just read the next question out for you. "It is believed that Srinivasa Ramanujan could write mathematical equations as if he had access to the whole universe. He also says that the goddess dictates those mathematical ideas to him. How can I reach that state?"

Sadhguru: First you must find a goddess. You're interested in this question? Hello?

Audience: [*Murmurs "Yes" and "No"*]

Sadhguru: I want to hear whatever I hear loudly, I'll go by that.

Audience: [*Shouts out "Yes" and "No"*]

Sadhguru: "No" is coming late. "Yes" came strong. [*Cheers*] All of you, do you use a phone?

Audience: Yes.

Sadhguru: Why do you use a phone? Why did we first of all make a telephone? Because we can speak. If we had no ability to speak, would we manufacture a microphone, a telephone, or any of these things? Why did we come up with a bicycle? Because we can walk. But we wanted to walk faster, so we ran. We ran and we knew there is a limit. We wanted to go faster than that, so we came up with a bicycle. Suppose we were made like a tree, rooted to one place, would we have invented a bicycle?

Audience: No.

Sadhguru: So a telephone, a telescope, a microscope, bicycle, automobiles, airplanes, everything – we want to enhance what faculties we already have. We did not suddenly come up with any machine for which we had no faculty, because we don't even know what those things are. Yes? The faculties that we do not have, we have no way to perceive whether they exist or not. We are only trying to take far the faculties that we have.

In this effort, we came up with many machines. All machines here are only enhancing our existing faculties. They have not come up with any absolutely new faculty. In the same context, right from ancient times in this culture, we came up with machines not made of material or a mechanical process, but an energetic process. What does a machine with an energetic process mean? See, suppose somebody is dead. Have you seen any dead people?

Audience: Yes.

Sadhguru: Where did you see? I never saw. You saw dead people or dead bodies?

Audience: Dead bodies.

Sadhguru: Ah. Dead body means what? Let's say, somebody just suffocated and died. Their heart was doing well – maybe not beating, but it was fit. Liver, kidney, everything was all okay. All the mechanical parts are okay. Only thing is, the person is not alive. That life energy is missing. So, this [*referring to oneself*] is also an energy machine on one level, isn't it so? Yes or no?

Audience: Yes.

Sadhguru: This is also an energy machine. On top of it we have put mechanical parts to it. Even if all the mechanical parts are intact, if there is no energy, this will not function. So from looking deep inside, we understood we could create an energetic machine without mechanical parts – because mechanical parts need a certain level of maintenance, servicing, and the works. But if you just create an energy machine, it will simply function day and night.

Let's say your phone was just an energy machine without mechanical parts – see, it's happening. From such a big phone, it's slowly becoming smaller, smaller. With lesser and lesser mechanical parts, it's becoming more and more efficient. Why do you think? Slowly it is moving towards a space where it is becoming more energetic than mechanical, isn't it so? Do you remember the old James Bond movies? Such a big phone! Ah, it was looking like a just-born baby. [*Laughs*] But today it's become so small.

They are expecting in another probably ten, fifteen years, your phone can be just imprinted on your hand. Simply like this [*holds hand up next to his face*] you can speak. Or you don't even have to do this. If you simply wave it around, it will say what you want it to say. From being mechanical, now we are going towards an energy-based machine. From a huge earthmover to a computer, this is the big difference – that it's more energetic and less mechanical.

So we created energy machines, for which the English word is "deity". Generally in this culture, we called them as *murtis*. These are forms – energetic forms which have a certain ability to do certain things. Different forms are like windows to the existence; you could open up different dimensions. All this has been forgotten, made into absolute nonsense today in the form of superstitions. Otherwise it was clearly prescribed. Today people get identified with this or that. They think it is about belonging to their gods. No, "god" is a wrong word for this – these are deities or murtis created with a specific purpose.

If you want intelligence, you go to one kind of deity. If you have fear problems, you go to another kind of deity. You have love issues, you go to another kind of deity. You have prosperity issues, you go to another kind of deity. Like this they made energetic forms which you must learn to use. These are not places of prayer. These are not places of worship. These are places where you learn how to use the machine for your benefit. They were built in various forms and various capacities. They were also connected to people's genetic information, which we called *Kula Devas*, where it works only for that genetic pool.

This is a very complex process. So, Ramanujan comes from the south. Why I am specially mentioning the south is… These things were there everywhere in the country, but the northern belt of this nation has taken too many invasions, too much disruption. South of the Vindhyas, we have been very well protected. Even today we maintain many things. We never had major disruptions as the north had. Because of this, certain sciences are still alive and active, which could produce a Ramanujan.

Ramanujan made mathematics for black holes more than a hundred years ago when there was no concept of black holes. Science always progresses like this: first the concept, then the theory, and then the mathematics. But he made the mathematics first, before there was a concept or theory. He was sitting on his death bed, and simply pouring out notebooks and notebooks of mathematics. People asked, "Where is this coming from? What is this?"

He said, "My Devi bleeds mathematics." [*Applause*]

Pranit: So Sadhguru, with your due permission, now we open the floor to the audience for asking the questions. Mic runners, kindly reach out to the people.

Sadhguru: I have heard of kite runners, where are these mic runners? Yeah, please [*pointing to the member of the audience who has the mic*].

Azeem: Namaskaram, Sadhguru.

Sadhguru: Hey, how come you got a better microphone than me, hm? [*Laughter*]

Azeem: My name is Azeem. I am a first-year student pursuing BCom Honors. So basically, we all know that at this age we get into a relationship, then we break up. One of my friends recently broke up, and he asked me to give him some advice on how to move on and how to cope with things. Being of the same age, I cannot advise him because I don't know how to move on. So, my question is, how to move on after that situation? [*Applause*]

Sadhguru: Well, somebody else has moved on. Even if you stay in the same place, distance will happen. See, let us understand this in terms of life – not in terms of trend, morality, right and wrong, but in terms of life. Azeem, do you remember what your great-great-great-ten-generations-ago-grandfather looked like?

Azeem: No.

Sadhguru: No. But his nose is sitting on your face. Yes or no?

Azeem: Yes.

Sadhguru: So is it true that your body has a tremendous amount of memory?

Azeem: Yes.

Sadhguru: This memory is on many different levels. There is an evolutionary memory. There is a genetic memory. There is a karmic memory. There are conscious levels of memory and unconscious levels of memory, articulate and inarticulate levels of memory. But if your great-grandfather's nose has to sit on your face, obviously your body is carrying a very complex mechanism of memory, isn't it?

Azeem: Yes.

Sadhguru: So, if this body is capable of such a complex sense of memory, you think it is not gathering memory with whatever you touch and feel and relate with? You think so or no?

Azeem: Yes.

Sadhguru: It does. It is gathering an enormous amount of memory – this is how you know. See, how to go up the steps, how to go down the steps – it looks very simple, but it's not simple; it's very complex. Your body has to remember. Otherwise it cannot go up and go down so simply. Well, today the sports people are talking about muscle memory, building memory into their system so that the sport can be executed at a certain level of efficiency. So this is not only for sports or a specific activity; every day you are imbibing so much memory. If there is a certain kind of congruence and cohesiveness to this memory, it will become productive. If there is a certain level of chaos to this memory, then you may know everything, but this memory will work against you because it's contradictory and conflicting within itself. When your friend asked you this question, the question itself is coming because it matters, isn't it?

Azeem: Yes.

Sadhguru: If it didn't matter, you could have just forgotten about it and gone on like an old pair of shoes. But it matters. Because you invested your thought, your emotion, and maybe even your body in it. Once you invested these three things, there is a profound sense of memory about that. If you create a lot of contradictory memory in your system, you will see life will tell you later – that you have everything, but you feel like you have nothing. Because it's confused and it's joyless, it doesn't have exuberance.

It's very important that young people understand the mechanism of what you have been given. If this was just a lump of flesh, you could have done whatever the hell you wanted with it. But this is a very sophisticated machine. If you treat it sensitively, it can do things in a phenomenal way; otherwise it will do mediocre things. Let's say you know nothing about computers and I gave you an Apple Air. Have you seen this model?

Azeem: Yeah.

Sadhguru: Very thin and sharp. I gave you this, but you don't know what it is. You took it home and started chopping cucumbers. It works very well. But isn't it a tragedy that you are using a computer to chop cucumber? Nothing wrong with the cucumber but something definitely wrong with you, isn't it?

Audience: Yes.

Sadhguru: Something very fundamentally wrong with you when you do not understand the significance of what you have on your hands – all significant things will go waste. I am saying, before you touch or involve yourself in anything, not just other human beings, you must see what is the level of involvement you wish for. You must see where you want to take this and also see what are the different impacts it will have upon you. You must consider whether this will work well for this life or work against this life. Otherwise you will become a loose life. I am not using the word "loose" in terms of morality. I am just talking about loose in terms of not being able to fulfil the direction in which you *wish* to go in your life. Bringing some integrity to your life – intellectual integrity, emotional integrity and physical integrity – is very, very, important. Well, beyond that if something goes wrong, you just have to understand, when you were born you came alone and when you die you will go alone.

Azeem: Thank you so much. [*Applause*]

Sadhguru: [*Pointing to someone in the audience*] Hey, this girl, she can't live without asking the question. Please give it to her.

Shriram: Mic runners, please. This side.

Sadhguru: Pranit, be a gentleman. Run and give her the microphone.

Shraddha: Thank you so much, Sadhguru, thank you. Namaskaram. I am Shraddha, Sadhguru. And very, very fortunate to have been a student of Isha Home School*.

Sadhguru: Oh! You? Okay. [*Laughs*]

Shraddha: So, my question is, I am pursuing science, and when I talk about Yoga and doing Shambhavi** in my college, people kind of look down upon me, saying, "You are a science student, how can you talk about these things?"

Sadhguru: [*Laughs*] How can you live sensibly? [*Sarcastically*]

Shraddha: [*Laughs*] So in my first year, I used to feel very bad about it, but then I just left it. Now I have a question as to why there is such resistance in the youth about our own sciences. I mean Indian sciences have been established by a deep understanding of everything. Why is there a resistance? And is it important that we convert this resistance into acceptance or, at least, you know, tell them not to disregard it without having explored it in its complete sense. And if so, how do we integrate inner sciences into the current education system that is in place? Thank you so much. [*Applause*]

Sadhguru: But Shraddha, why are you doing science in a commerce college?

Shraddha: I am from a different college.

Sadhguru: Okay. See, unfortunately today, we have a constipated perception of what is science or what is scientific. Essentially the way science or the scientific process is defined is

---

* School founded by Sadhguru at Isha Yoga Center.
** Shambhavi Mahamudra Kriya, an inner energy process.

if there is a systematic approach to it, and the approach should be repeatable and should work not just for me but for many people. Then it is considered a science. Science is fundamentally physics, but there are other sciences which have evolved out of it. Biological studies, psychological studies and social sciences are there. So anything which has a systematic approach and is applicable not just to one person but to a larger number of people becomes a science or a scientific approach.

In that sense, there is no other science which is as largely applicable as the Yogic sciences. It is just that the Yoga that people have heard about today is a rebound from the American coast, so they think Yoga means wearing Lulu pants and going around. It's a kind of fashion. No. I want you to listen to this carefully because this is not something that you can explore in a casual atmosphere like this. Yoga literally means union. What does union mean? The very body that you carry right now, one day somebody is going to bury you or burn you. Smoking or non-smoking, we will do it. Either we do this or that – will you become part of the earth?

Audience: Yes.

Sadhguru: How come *now* you are not part of it? Even now you are part of it, isn't it? You're just a small outcrop of this earth. Only because you were given the ability to be mobile, you lost your sense. You thought you are a world by yourself. If you were stuck like a tree, I am sure you would have understood you are a part of the earth, isn't it? Just because the planet gave you the freedom to move, how stupid we became. It's not just with body, it is so with the entire universe. It is not just with the physical form, it is so with every aspect of you.

So Yoga means union. It is a science of how to obliterate the boundaries of your individuality so that you become a much larger life than you are right now. Either you can live here as a constipated life… When I say "a constipated life", constipation means it happens little by little. Right now, for most people, life is happening little by little. You ask them what are the great moments in their life, they say, "When I passed my examination, I felt great. Then I was miserable. Then I found a job, I felt great. But then, you know, all the people made me miserable. Then, I got married, it was really wonderful. Then my mother-in-law came and *pishoow* [*gestures it being extinguished*]." [*Laughter*] She didn't come – she was there all the time, before you and your man. "But… " like this it goes on. They will count five things where they had great moments in their life – this is a constipated life where every moment of your life is not an exuberant outburst of life. It is *once* in a way that something happens to you. Constipated or no?

Audience: Yes.

Sadhguru: Do you want to live a constipated life?

Audience: No.

Sadhguru: If you have to live an exuberant life, the boundaries of individuality have to be erased to whatever extent. Only then you capture a larger amount of life and you have a larger experience of life, a higher level of exuberance than what you normally see around you. Have you blown soap bubbles, at least when you were young?

Audience Members: Yes… Now also we are young…

Sadhguru: Oh! Did you blow soap bubbles at least when you were *children*?

Audience: Yes!

Sadhguru: So you got only this tiny bubble. But somebody else got such a big bubble. Same soap, but somebody blows this big of a bubble, but yours is only this much. You also have a lungful of air, you also have soap. Why do you think it happens? Because if you want to expand boundaries, what is important is not the desire. What is important is you need to capture that much air in that limited possibility. Then it becomes that big.

Similarly, this one [*referring to oneself*]. See, my body and your body are different. This is me, that is you. Till we get buried we don't understand it's all the same earth. But right now, this is my body, that is your body, one hundred percent clear. This is my mind and that's your mind, hundred percent clear. This can't be that, that can't be this. But there is no such thing as my life and your life. There is just life.

How much *life* you capture, not how much information you capture, determines the scope and scale of your life. If this has to happen, you have to breach the concretized boundaries of your individuality and push it. When the boundaries are dissolved, then we say you are in Yoga. If one experiences that dissolution, then we refer to that person as a Yogi. Well, how far each individual is going to go is subject to various realities. But should you not at least make an effort, a scientific and focused effort as to how to breach these boundaries of individuality which we ourselves created? Hello?

Audience: Yes.

Sadhguru: All your boundaries are created by you, isn't it? You create the boundary and you suffer the boundary. What kind of life is that? If nature created the boundary and you're suffering that, that's understandable. You create your own boundary because of self-preservation. In pursuit of self-preservation you build walls. These walls of self-preservation will become walls of self-imprisonment. If you don't want that, you need Yoga.

"Oh, should I twist, should I turn, should I stand on my head?" No. Yoga does not mean twisting, turning. You can breathe and do Yoga. You can walk and do Yoga. You can talk and do Yoga. You can read and do Yoga. You can sleep and do Yoga. You can stand and do Yoga. You can do Yoga in whichever way! There is no specific activity; it's a certain dimension. What is a dimension – once it goes to the United States, unfortunately they reduce it into a specific activity, and you have to wear Lululemon pants. Otherwise, no Yoga.

Yesterday somebody asked me, "Sadhguru, how many hours of Yogasanas do *you* do?"

I said, "Twenty seconds!"

"What!? Only twenty seconds?"

"Yes." Actually, it's true. I wake up in the morning, if I sit up, just twenty seconds, I'm done. Then, do I not do Yoga the rest of the day? No! I live Yoga. Because my entire life is to constantly wipe away the boundaries within myself and within everybody else. This is Yoga. What we are doing here is Yoga right now. [*Applause*]

Shriram: We'll be taking two more questions.

Shudipto: Hello sir, myself Shudipto Das. [*Reading the question from his phone*] So, I saw one of your videos on what a twenty-year-old should do in life. There you asked us to take a few days off uninfluenced by anybody and think what is needed the most for the universe. But also you added…

Sadhguru: Where are you? [*Audience members point to Shudipto*] Oh, okay, fine. Yeah.

Shudipto: …so should I repeat?

Sadhguru: No, no, I got it. But why are you copying a question? [*Referring to his question being read*]

Shudipto: No, no. I'll ask you my question. So you added to keep aside the things that are coming due to our immediate compulsions. Suppose my immediate compulsions are shelter and to get self-sufficiency, how do I keep them aside and work on something as important as, say, gender equality?

Sadhguru: Oh, what is that? What do you do about gender equality?

Shudipto: Like I feel that there should be gender equality, and in this stage of the world such a situation is not present.

Sadhguru: No, you don't have to do anything about gender equality. If you don't mess with the girls, they will prove they are equal. [*Applause*] Unfortunately, many times, they will prove they are a little more than you. [*Applause*] No, I don't know how these two things are linked, but you are talking about what I said, that before you take major steps in your life, you must move to a place where you are not influenced by your peers, your elders, your parents, your teachers. Spend some time upon yourself: "What is it that I want to do with this life?" This life [*referring to oneself*]. Do not understand life as job, food, profession, this, that, nonsense. *This one* is life, isn't it? You are mistaking the accessories of life as life, unfortunately.

Today, if people say "my life", we are supposed to understand they are talking about their car, their home, their wife or husband, their dog. No, *this one* is life. Those are all accessories of life. Once the accessories of life become more significant than life itself – oh, you are finished, okay? Whatever you do, you will be messed up. So I said, withdraw from all the influences that you have. If you think you are a worthwhile life, it deserves attention, isn't it? You spend a few days looking at it. If all these people were not there telling you a thousand things as to what you should do, what is it that *you* really want to do – you must look at it, isn't it?

People who have been married for thirty-five years come and tell me, "Sadhguru, I knew I made a mistake with this marriage."

Then I ask, "Really, then how did you get these three children? If marriage was a mistake, you could have stopped right there. How did three children happen?"

"No, Sadhguru, you know…"

I *know* how that happens. [*Laughter*] "But then, how did you build this big house, this nonsense, and all the things you are beginning to suffer now, unfortunately. You are not enjoying them, you are suffering them. So, how did you do all this?"

"No, Sadhguru, you know, mistake, mistake, mistake, mistake."

Why are you a serial mistake? Because you don't stop and look – what is it that this life really cares for. Beyond social pressures, beyond teachings, beyond all kinds of diktats that come from everywhere, what is it that this life wants? Every human being *must* look at it. It's everybody's right to look at it, beyond all the pressures. [*Applause*]

Shriram: Someone, please… from that side. This will be the last question for the day.

Lavanya: Namaskaram, Sadhguru. I am Lavanya. I am studying Economics Honors, first year. I am from Hyderabad. Despite being surrounded by so many people, we still lack that feeling of belonging to somebody, being accepted by somebody, being loved by somebody. How should we deal with that discontent and loneliness?

Sadhguru: [*Speaking in Telugu*] *Yemmandi, Hyderabad nunchi vacchi?* (What, coming from Hyderabad?)… [*Lavanya laughs*] See, you must understand this. Right now in these two hours, you are speaking two different tongues. On one level, many questions are aimed towards "How can I be free from this and that?" On another level, you are asking, "How can I bind myself to something or somebody?" You must decide, what is the highest value in your life – freedom or bondage? Please, I would like to hear that word.

Audience: [*Shouts in unison*] Freedom!

Sadhguru: Oh, freedom! But if you are free, you feel lost. If you go into the mountains and you are totally free – that is, nobody around, nothing around, you are just in the empty space of the mountains – you don't feel free, you think you are lost. So, handling freedom requires a certain clarity and strength. Most people cannot handle freedom. They are always trying to bind themselves, but only talking, mouthing freedom all the time. If you really set them free, they will suffer immensely. So, this is an evolutionary issue, in the sense, human beings are right now like a caged bird. If you keep a bird caged for a long period of time and then, one day, you take off the door of the cage, the bird will still not fly. From inside it'll protest that it's not free, but it'll not fly. Human condition is just that.

For all other creatures, nature has drawn two lines within which they have to live and die, and that's what they do. But only for human beings, there is only a bottom line, there is no top line. And that's what they are suffering. If their life was also fixed like every other creature's life, they wouldn't be stressed, they wouldn't be anxious, they wouldn't be struggling about how to handle their own intelligence. And that is what you are seeking unknowingly. You may seek it in the form of relationships, you may seek it in the form of profession, you may seek it in the form of nationality, ethnicity, community, God, heaven, hell.

All you are trying to do is draw an artificial line that does not exist. Because freedom needs courage, freedom needs a certain madness. If you are very sane, you cannot be free because you will go between the two lines of logic. To be free, it takes a lot of strength. First of all, what needs to happen if you want to be free is... Do you understand that all human experience has a chemical basis to it?

Audience: Yes.

Sadhguru: What you call joy is one kind of chemistry, misery is another kind of chemistry. Stress is one kind of chemistry, anxiety another kind of chemistry. Agony one kind of chemistry, ecstasy another kind of chemistry. At least you know ecstasy is another kind of chemistry, I hear. [*Laughs*] So, your experience of life has a chemical basis to it. This is the most superficial way of looking at it. There are other dimensions to it, but for your understanding, in other words, you are a chemical soup. The question is only, are you a great soup or a lousy soup?

If you have a chemistry of blissfulness, then if you close your eyes, it's fantastic; if you open your eyes, it's fantastic; if somebody is here, it's fantastic; nobody is here, it's very fantastic. But you have a lousy chemistry. If you look at them and they smile at you, it's nice – not fantastic. If they glare at you, suddenly it's a problem. If these people are happening just the way you want, your chemistry is *reasonably* balanced. If they do something that you don't like, *boom*! It goes somewhere else. So, essentially, you have not looked at this mechanism, what is the basis of this, how it functions, how you can make it function at its highest level.

Right now, let's say you're really blissed out like me – do you care who is around, who is not around? If they are around, it's fantastic. They're gone – fantastic. Because your experience of life is no more determined by what you have and what you don't have, whether it's people or things or food or this or that. Once your way of being is not determined by anything outside of you, then there is no such thing as loneliness, but you will enjoy your aloneness. At this young age, it's a little difficult to understand this – whether you like it or you don't like it, within this body you are *always* alone, isn't it? Whether you do interaction or intercourse or whatever, you are still alone in this body. Yes or no?

Audience: Yes.

Sadhguru: If you don't learn how to handle this aloneness, you have not learnt anything about life. The most beautiful thing about life is nobody can get here [*points within*]. It's just my space. Nobody can invade me. They can capture me, they can torture me, they can do so many things, but they cannot invade me because I have a space which is just my own. Isn't this the most wonderful aspect of your life? Don't suffer that. That is the most beautiful thing. Oh, but you want to pine a little romantically and enjoy... What are those popular songs? Pining for somebody, "Without you I cannot exist." [*Laughter*]

Riya: Most of the songs are that way now.

Sadhguru: Sing one song, no. [*Laughter*] Older ones, older ones.

Riya: I am horrible at singing.

Sadhguru: Just tell me the words, I will sing.

Audience: [*Calls out lyrics*]

Sadhguru: Say it on the microphone.

Pranit: [*Speaking in Hindi*] *Hum tere bin ab reh nahi sakte, tere bina kya vajood mera?* (I can't live without you. Who am I without you?) [*Applause*]

Sadhguru: You're saying it to me? [*talking to Pranit*] [*Laughter*]

Pranit: [*Laughs and shakes his head*]

Riya: Shriram is a singer.

Sadhguru: Shriram, that song... what he is saying...

Shriram: [*Sings in Hindi*] *Hum tere bin ab reh nahi sakte, tere bina kya vajood mera?* [*Cheers*]

Sadhguru: See, all the boys must learn songs like this, otherwise you can't floor the girls. [*Laughter*] But the girls should understand the guy has a need and he is doing this. It's not really true but let's enjoy the game right now. [*Applause*] Because what we do is just a certain game – life is, because it comes to an end. But the important thing is how you are within yourself. If you are here in such a way that you are only driven by your needs, you will live a very meager life. But if you can sit here without any need but you will do whatever is needed, then you will live a magnificent life. It's my wish and my blessing every one of you must have a fantastic life. Make it happen for yourself. [*Applause*]

Shriram: Thank you so much, Sadhguru, for all the insights you have seeded in our minds. We'll *try* to incorporate those in our day-to-day lives.

Sadhguru: Hey, when this Shriram guy sings, girls, please know he is just a singer. [*Laughter*] He doesn't mean it, I mean to say. Thank you, thank you very much.

THE BEGINNINGS

In August 2018, students of Shri Ram College of Commerce, New Delhi, were busy Googling details of a public figure that they were familiar with, but didn't know enough about. His YouTube videos were doing rounds on WhatsApp and WeChat groups on the campus. SRCC's notice boards were plastered with images of him on an adventure motorcycle, and a black and white stamp-sized logo – "Youth and Truth - Unplug with Sadhguru". The unusually high level of excitement and interest was evoked not only by his stature, popularity, and the impact his talk was likely to have, but also the fact that he was going to be in a freewheeling conversation with three SRCC students.

Coincidently, at the same time a year ago, to revitalize India's severely depleting rivers, Sadhguru had kickstarted the mammoth *Rally for Rivers* movement from Isha Yoga Center at Coimbatore, which culminated in New Delhi on 2 October 2017. Conversely, in 2018, New Delhi was playing host for the launch of *Youth and Truth*. SRCC students had the distinct privilege of being at the first *Youth and Truth* dialogue, which would set a precedence for many more that would follow in the next three weeks.

"It was going to be one of the largest events on campus during my time here as a student," says Pranit, one of the moderators.

Another moderator shares, "We have hosted many popular public figures at our campus, but this was different because here we had an opportunity to sit next to Sadhguru and pose our most audacious questions. It was hard to believe that I was free to ask him whatever I wished. In college, we are used to lectures and monologues, but an event like this was unheard of, especially with a spiritual leader."

THE CHOSEN ONES

On one hand, while Isha volunteers were busy crafting an online and offline campaign of immense magnitude to present a completely different facet of their Guru to the world (and especially to the youth), on the other hand, the students of SRCC, the crème de la crème of Delhi University, were busy partaking in a competition of a different kind.

"When we got to know that our college was going to host Sadhguru for this new series, everybody wanted to participate and help organize. The faculty was really involved, and they created a rigorous competition to select student representatives," explains one of the students who was involved in organizing the event.

The task of shortlisting three student-moderators from around 3000 wasn't an easy one. Neither was the shortlisting of questions. Almost every student had a question to ask. Questions were collected from social media platforms affiliated with the college, including various student associations and forums, Google forms, and other offline means. After multiple sessions and competitions, twelve students were selected, and fifty questions were shortlisted from a pool of over a thousand.

Isha volunteers then conducted elaborate workshops to understand students' perspectives of Sadhguru and alleviate their apprehension about asking taboo questions. Swami Sukhada from Isha Yoga Center played an important role in helping the students. "Every city and college has a distinct culture that triggers certain types of questions. The questions also surface from the personalities of those posing them. So, we wanted to assess what kind of questions the students are likely to pose," he shares. "One of the quirkiest questions from the SRCC students," he adds, "was about why Sadhguru sits the way he does. There were multiple theories and explanations floating among the students."

At the end of the workshop, both the questions and the panellists were finalized, and the stage was set.

A DAY TO REMEMBER

On 4 September 2018, excitement was palpable in the SRCC air. The response to the event was so great that just a few days before the big day, the venue was changed to the larger sports auditorium. Despite the eleventh-hour changes to accommodate a huge audience, things had surprisingly not devolved into utter chaos. "While many events at SRCC hold massive student crowds, this crowd was more diverse and very well-managed," says a student who was at the talk. The celebratory atmosphere was so contagious – students were dancing to the beats of drums outside the auditorium even before Sadhguru arrived.

Meanwhile, the three chosen ones, collectively decked in tricolor (of India's national flag), were getting ready for their meeting with Sadhguru in the green room. "It was definitely a whole new experience. And also my first time wearing a kurta!" recalls Pranit. The meeting with Sadhguru really helped break the ice for all the panellists and made them comfortable enough to banter onstage. "We were not only representing SRCC, but also the entire Delhi University. So there was a lot of pressure to carry that legacy, deliver well on stage, and not disappoint our institute. In the end, it all went really well. We received a lot of appreciation from everyone on campus," he shares on behalf of the moderator trio.

While all went well during the course of the event, Isha volunteers were in for a surprise after the talk. An informal frisbee match with Sadhguru drew a sea of students as far as the eye could see. The sheer sight of Sadhguru lost amidst the masses was eye-opening and somewhat alarming for the organizers who realized subsequent events would need to take into account crowd management at all times. Swami Sukhada says, "For the first time we realized that Sadhguru has a huge fanbase across all kinds of audiences, including people who have no interest in Yoga or spirituality. SRCC students were sharing how cool Sadhguru was! He was received like a rock star."

"If the world was guided by youth, it would be a better place. They are the ones who are most alive, idealistic, and energetic."

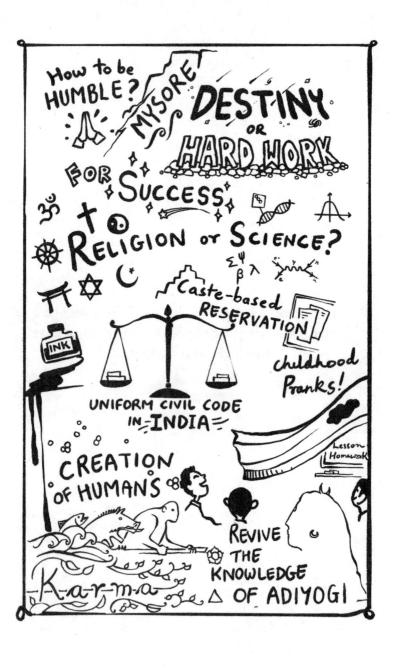

REGIONAL INSTITUTE OF EDUCATION, MYSURU

Demonstration Multipurpose School
15 September 2018

Sadhguru: Hello. I've never been more embarrassed in my life that someone like CGN Sir* is trying to come and touch my feet. [*Laughter*] Please don't do this to me. It's a privilege that I can be here. My memory is not in terms of words but always in terms of visuals, smells and sounds. In this playground, things that have happened, almost everything is live for me right now. [*Pointing behind him*] This was our escape route to Bogadi Lake. [*Applause*]

Ms Sarasa: Hello. I have no words. [*Speaking to the audience*] If you see me here facing you, it's a miracle. And I have the

---

* Retired Headmaster C.G. Nagaraj of Demonstration Multipurpose School, who bowed to Sadhguru before the talk.

privilege to talk to Sadhguru in my own way so that you will also get a different idea about another area. Namaskar, Sadhguru. [*Applause*] You are back in the campus after almost fifty years.

Sadhguru: Forty-five.

Ms Sarasa: Forty-five years. What does it feel like to be back? What do you recall about your school? What is it that inspired you? What is it that you disapprove of? Can you tell us something?

Sadhguru: Well, no school kept me for more than one year. This is one school which kept me for two years. [*Applause*] So, I'm grateful for that.

I have to admit I was not much of a student. [*Laughs*] I *did* come to school whenever it was a must. [*Laughter*] Like you saw the rap*, they're all doing *poochu poochu* and all that. So, by the time I was seven, eight years of age, I had a dark cloud of a billion questions around my head. And the chatter that would be going on in the world around me – parents, siblings, friends, even school – it was almost like a second channel. The first channel was my own endless questions.

It came to a point that by the time I was fourteen or fifteen, I was almost kind of thinking these questions will never be answered. Because at least with my limited exposure at that time, I turned to wherever people usually said the answers were. But all those answers were readymade answers, not something that people felt as a live experience. Something that they have read

---

* Referring to the promotional rap song for *Youth and Truth*, "*Poochu Kya?*", where youth ask questions that are considered taboo.

somewhere, something that they heard somewhere, somebody said something. And all the guys who are supposed to have known were dead.

So, I'm sorry, but it was only one small part of me that was attending school. Rest of me was just continuously lost. So, the best thing about the school for me was the open space, the trees, the Bogadi Lake, and the fish in the Bogadi Lake. It nourished us. [*Laughs*] Probably in Mysore City, this was the only school with so much acreage and trees.

I think you people have already researched and seen that I never got anywhere beyond 37 ever in my report cards. [*Laughter*] There are some of my friends here [*pointing towards the audience*] who were part of the scenery there. We always walked out of the examination hall within thirty minutes, because thirty minutes was mandatory. [*Laughter*] I calculated 36, 37 – and I'm out. So, you will see my marks card is always less than 38, not more, because that's all I wrote for. I know this is not an inspiring thing to say to the students here, but the education was just a sideline in my mind. I knew I didn't want to be left out in the previous class. I wanted to go with my friends, so I kept going to the next class. That's about it.

Those who were closely around me would know that I did not have textbooks, I did not have notes, I did not have guides. Education occupied a very small portion of my mind, because just about everything interested me. I was made like this: If I see a leaf, I could spend six, seven hours just looking at the leaf. I spent days and days just looking at the mechanics of an ant. Still did not figure how the hell it works. [*Laughs*] Sat up in the nights just staring at the darkness for whole nights sometimes.

I was a kind of an absentee student even when I was physically present, because it started happening to me very early that there were many channels of thought going on in my mind. I would be thinking about fifteen things continuously at the same time. Even now my mind works like this; otherwise all the activity wouldn't be happening. I spent so much time with the nature of my own body and my own mind. I would be fully engaged with what's happening here, but I would be thinking of ten other things at the same time continuously.

So, I'm not saying this because I'm here now... but every year I was in different schools. The very fact that I spent two years in this school, I enjoyed this school the most.

Ms Sarasa: Thank you.

Sadhguru: The best part of it was the activity because it was a multipurpose school. [*Applause*] I hope it's still that way. We didn't have to sit in the classroom all the time. There was so much activity. And I see a lot of eucalyptus trees now, but there were some large trees at that time. The trees and the space were the main things that brought me here every day. Otherwise, I would get lost halfway somewhere. And about the school, what do I remember? Just everything.

I met somebody from the school about three years ago; he has become a chartered accountant in Bangalore. And just like that I was parking my car, and he was getting out of his car, smoking a cigarette. I got out and said "Hey", and I called him by his name as I would have spoken to him at the school. Because for me, these last forty years feel like a few days. That's how rapidly it's gone. So, I spoke to him just as I would have at school and he was surprised. "Oh, you... you've become a guru... oh, oof."

He put the cigarette down and stamped it out. Then he didn't know what to say. He pulled out his cigarette pack and said, "Do you smoke?" [*Laughter*]

I said, "No."

"Oh, you don't smoke? You don't drink?"

"I drink water." [*Laughter*] That's a basic drink everybody is supposed to drink. And, I mean, I just noticed that he is pretty successful, everything is fine. Only thing is life has become tepid.

When I was in school, for many days I wouldn't utter a word, because when you don't know anything, what the hell is there to say? That's one thing I realized very early, that I don't know a damn thing in the universe. I simply paid attention, paid attention, paid attention because I did not know one thing from the other. Maybe I would have looked withdrawn to people, but I was not really withdrawn. I was exuberantly alive within myself. But because I was just drinking in the world, I had nothing to say because I did not know anything.

So, not knowing anything, naturally I became super attentive, not in the classes but to the world. I noticed every small thing. It looks funny to people, but if I close my eyes, I can tell you on a particular day what kind of flowers were blooming in front of the school, what kind of garden they had at that time, how the bus was parked, how always this driver would start on the second gear, instead of the first gear. [*Laughter*] That old Leyland bus – you remember, all of you? The old, fancy-looking body [*motions with his hands to show a curve*]. Like this, I noticed, "Oh, today he's starting the bus on second gear, the fool."

I'm like this. So, what is that specific thing? No. I just remember everything, which is embarrassing for me because I was not a great student. [*Laughs*]

Ms Sarasa: Agree, agree. We are a part of the whole environment. Now, your caption "Youth and Truth" is very captivating. Can you tell us how we can make the kids sensitive to being truthful? This is something very intriguing. We can punish them, and for the fear of punishment they might run away, but that doesn't ensure they will be truthful. If a kid is made truthful in the younger days, the adult automatically will be truthful. Can you tell us how we parents and teachers can make them truthful?

Sadhguru: Well, when we say "Youth and Truth", we are not talking about being verbally truthful or not truthful. People go about propounding this in many different ways. To put it very simply, what works in all levels of life must be the truth, isn't it? Hello?

Audience: Yes.

Sadhguru: What works on *all* levels of life must be the truth. Somebody said, "Satyamev Jayate." Well, this was said in the Upanishads that "only truth works" – that's what it means. Mahatma Gandhi used it in a political way during the independence struggle. It worked well for him. But now we are living in the twenty-first century; saying "only truth works" will make people frown.

So, I'm putting it the other way around. What genuinely works on all levels of life must be the truth. What is it that works on all levels of life? See, no matter what the nature of activity you take up, what arena of life you enter into, it's important that a human being knows that human experience is essentially generated from within. Whether it is anger or hatred or love or compassion, peacefulness, tranquility, turmoil, stress, anxiety, madness, agony, ecstasy – every human experience happens from within. At least, what's happening from within us must happen the way we want it. Do you agree with me? What's happening around us will never happen a hundred percent our way. Those of you who are married, even if you are just two people at home, even then it doesn't happen hundred percent your way. If it happens fifty-one percent your way, you have the controlling stake – you must be happy. Hundred percent your way, nobody is going to live with you.

The outside world is never ever going to happen a hundred percent your way. And I'm glad it is so. Because if everything happened your way, where the hell do I go? [*Laughter*] So, a little bit my way, little bit your way, little bit somebody else's way. This is the nature of the world, and it's fine. But what happens within me must happen my way. If what happens within me doesn't happen my way and just about anybody can take over anytime, then this is the worst form of slavery, isn't it? Somebody can decide what should happen within you. Isn't this the most horrible way to live? All the romantic people are not saying anything. [*Laughter*]

This is one truth, that what happens within you must be determined by you. If you are determining what should happen within you, would you choose to be blissful or miserable? You must choose right now; I'm going to bless you.

Audience: Blissful.

Sadhguru: That is only twelve people. If you have a choice between being blissful and miserable, what's your choice for yourself?

Audience: Blissful!

Sadhguru: What you want for your neighbor may be debatable [*audience laughs*], but what you want for yourself is hundred percent clear, isn't it? You want the highest level of pleasantness. There is substantial medical and scientific evidence to prove to you that your body and your brain will work at their best only when you're in a pleasant state of experience. All of you know this by experience, but today, unless it comes out of the lab, it's not true. So if you are right now blissed out – not because you've been up to something, but simply blissed out with life – if you are in a very pleasant state of experience, if someone comes in front of you, what will be the nature of your interaction or your behavior with that person? Pleasant or unpleasant?

Audience: Pleasant.

Sadhguru: Pleasant. When you're in a state of anger, resentment, frustration, misery, if somebody comes here, they will get a share of it. [*Laughter*] Will they or not?

Audience: Yes.

Sadhguru: So, if this one thing you take charge of in your life, that what happens within you is only determined by you, you will ensure that this one [*referring to oneself*] is always pleasant. If this one is pleasant, your body and your brain work at their best. In this physical world, whatever success you are seeking in whichever field, essentially it's about how well you harness this body and this brain, yes? If you know how to harness the prowess of this body and this mind, you are successful in the physical world.

Ms Sarasa: Wow. Can I take one more question?

Sadhguru: [*Indicating agreement*] Mmm.

Ms Sarasa: Now, in continuation with Sadhguru-ji, you said, "To be blissful is in our hands and we make misery out of it because…"

Sadhguru: No, no. To be miserable is also in our hands.

Ms Sarasa: In our hands, right. Now I'm going to another issue – the children making mistakes, scoring less, failing in the exam, coming home, and the parents feeling as though the sky has fallen. Now, how do we sensitize our parents? That it's okay to score less, it's okay to fail. The child will grow and live. How do we say this to our parents? [*Applause*]

Sadhguru: You should not send the marks cards home. [*Applause*] By the time I came to Demonstration School, I was a little evolved. That is, at least there were some numerals on my marks card. Before that, till my seventh standard, I consistently got six zeros in all the tests. [*Laughter*] Because I never wrote a word – nobody explained to me why the hell I should go to school. I just didn't understand why I was supposed to go there every day. So I went there, and an empty paper came. If they insisted, I wrote my name. Otherwise, I gave an empty paper without a name. So I got zero, zero, zero, zero… [*Laughs*]

I remember, when these marks cards were being given out, some students would be strutting around because they had come first, second, whatever. Some of those first, second students in Nirmala Convent also came to Demonstration School following me. And some of those children would be sitting and crying because they didn't have the numbers that they were supposed to have. I never once opened this card; I just took it and gave it to my father. I thought this is a transaction between the teacher and my father. [*Laughter*]

Ms Sarasa: Correct, correct.

Sadhguru: And every time I gave the marks card to him, my father would blow up and so many things would happen. The drama would continue for three days in the house. [*Laughter*] Before he used to go on night duty. Otherwise every day in the evening the drama would continue. It's very difficult to explain this – it's not like I was thinking he was angry with my marks. I just didn't understand the whole drama that was going on. I only gave it to him, and he was supposed to sign it, not me. [*Laughter*]

So, by the time I came to Demonstration School, I had understood that I needed to get some numbers there. It's not just me. I'm sure at least thirty to forty percent of the children have no clue why the hell they are going to school. [*Applause*]

Ms Sarasa: Right.

Sadhguru: Fortunately, this school has space and, you know, there is room and multiple activities. In most schools, it's just a concrete building where you have to go, sit and listen to these people who are reading something, and you are supposed to write that down. And everybody is supposed to clap their hands if you write the same things that they told you. [*Applause*] I'm saying this from my perspective at that time, not now. [*Laughter*] From the child's perspective, he doesn't know what this is all about. Parents keep asking, "Will you become a doctor or engineer?" How are these two things connected? [*Laughter*]

My father being a physician, after my twelfth standard they said, "You must do medicine." They said they could get me a seat in the Pune military college, even with my meager marks.

I said, "No."

Then they said, "Okay, at least apply for engineering."

I said, "See, this doesn't make sense to me. If I say 'no' to a doctor, tell me to become a veterinary doctor, Ayurvedic doctor, witch doctor – say something. But if I say 'no' to a doctor, you say, 'An engineer.' What is this?"

This is not even about education. This is a social issue. Unfortunately for most children in this country, their education is just a social phenomenon. It is not a learning process. It is not about enlarging their horizons. It's just about "My neighbor's son is a doctor. How do I tell him my son is just a clerk?" This is all the problem. [*Applause*]

If this problem has to go from this country, we have to do some serious work to place all professions on the same level. It's very important. [*Applause*] I'm not trying to disqualify the education system per se, but the way we are approaching it. It doesn't matter whether it's a carpenter or an electrician, a doctor or an engineer – all the professions are important for our well-being and survival.

See, you may go to a doctor and survive. But if you get into an autorickshaw which has a bad driver, you will not survive. So, I'm asking which profession is more important or less important? Why is one thing less important than the other? [*Applause*] To settle this socially, some economic parity needs to happen. Today, slowly it is happening – carpenters are earning more than doctors in India, which is a very good thing. Now you can expect some carpentry to happen in this country. Otherwise, the kind of carpenters you have right now… if he comes and fixes a door and you close it, you can't open it again. If you open it, you can't close it. [*Laughter*] This is the reality, and we are living with this as if it's all right. It's not all right.

If you want to have great carpenters, great electricians, great autorickshaw drivers, great teachers and great everything, it's very important that there is parity between all professions. One profession is seen like it's godlike and another profession is seen as nothing. So then, naturally, you produce substandard nonsense in the country.

This process of education, as we know it today, needs to change, but there are economic conditions in the country which you cannot ignore. So as a part of this, I unfolded three systems of education. There is something called Isha Vidhya, Isha Home School and Isha Samskriti.

Isha Vidhya was created for rural education. In rural Tamil Nadu, we are providing education that is as good as they would get in any good urban school. Forty percent of the children are first-generation schoolgoers. You should see their parents – they are all daily wage laborers, but their children speak fluent English. [*Applause*] They can handle computers by the time they're seven, eight years of age, and they're competent in many things. Their parents are amazed, it's like their children have become super-kids. But all that's happened is a few philanthropists and others are supporting. Right now over 9000 children are on full scholarship in these schools. [*Applause*]

Though there is other extra-curricular stuff, this education is mainly designed to get this population out of the social and economic pit in which they are. In the villages, I always notice this... After I left Mysore, I rode across India on my motorcycle. Simply, without any destination, till I hit the nation's borders. I turned around and went in another direction and another direction. I crisscrossed India for three continuous years. In one calendar year, I put in somewhere between 55,000 to 65,000 kilometers on 250cc, *doog, doog, doog...* you know, the Java. [*Applause*] And with the roads the way they were, I did some back-breaking riding. All I did was drink in the country. I saw the people in many ways. I went into villages and just stayed in any home which welcomed me. I ate with them, stayed with them for a night, and the next morning I left. Neither did they ask for my name, nor did I ask their name, but they welcomed me, they fed me, they allowed me to sleep in their house for one night before I left.

Children from the ages of three to ten, their eyes are like stars, and they are full of enthusiasm, full of life, jumping around. When you meet the same children when they are twelve to fourteen, they are downcast. You will see this everywhere in Indian villages. I thought, "Why have they become like this?" It's not that they don't have food to eat. It's just that somewhere in their minds they've realized that their life cannot be any better than the way it is right now. They know this is a trap. They might not have articulated this in their minds, but the realization has sunk in that this is all there is. A few people manage to remain enthusiastic and full on, but for nearly eighty percent of them, by the time they reach thirteen to fourteen years of age, their eyes have become dim.

So I thought we should start model schools in Tamil Nadu. Today we have nine schools. [*Applause*] The Isha teachers are crazy. The basic qualification is they must be crazy. [*Laughter*]

Crazy means they should not think, "What about me, what is my future, what is my career, when is my increment, where will I go, after retirement what will I do?" After retirement, you will die. So I want crazy people who are not thinking *where* they will go; they are just interested in doing what they have to do right now. I've found thousands of such people and I just managed to provide them a little bit of clothing and make sure they are well-nourished – that's about it. And keep them cranked up, full of enthusiasm. And I taught them something, that if they close their eyes, tears of ecstasy will come. On this it's all running. So this is rural education.

Then we started a Home School for the affluent children. Parents who are reasonably affluent, who went through the factory-kind of school system just to earn a living – some of them went outside the country and made money, some of them made money here – now they want their children to have something better than the way their education happened. For them, we created Isha Home School.

This system of education is like this: we built a large household where twenty children live along with two house parents who are dedicated people. The basic qualification is they should not be trained teachers. We have doctors, engineers, accountants, well-educated people, but they are not trained for teaching because we didn't want any systems there. We want the teacher to sit in the class not knowing a thing and willing to learn along with the student. It is an interaction, and a together-learning process for both.

Whether it's parents or teachers or us right now, the only thing is we came here a few years earlier than the so-called students or children. Just because we are here a few years early, we don't have to bully them every day. [*Applause*] See, people think bullying is happening with only first-year students in the school or college. No, it starts at home. Parents bully you, teachers bully – I am sorry, Maa [*to Ms Sarasa*]... [*Laughter*] You did not. When I say "bullying", the whole system is like that. A child's intelligence needs to be explored, but nobody has the time to do that because it's a mass of population.

In this school, I don't know, there are 700 to 800 children? In many schools, 3000 to 5000 children. In the government schools in Tamil Nadu alone, there are over a million children. Private schools have a similar number. So, two million children just in one state. How do you educate them? Obviously, it's a factory. But only if we can care for children like we do for a garden, then each one will blossom in their own way. But that is not possible on a large scale.

So, this Home School is exclusive. We take only 340 children. This is over a hundred acres of land, and we have 10,000 square kilometers of rainforest as our backyard. So, they have all the space that they need. It's a seven-day school. No holiday, because I don't think you need a break from learning. If you have stimulated the longing to know in a child, he doesn't want a break. The teachers know that there are four days for some activity. Suddenly one day it will not be classroom; it will be some activity. The children will never be told which day it is. That is their holiday. But activity days are busier than the classroom days. Because I don't think children need a break. They need a break from monotony. They don't need rest.

Today I see children are sitting like old people, their legs crossed, in a La-Z-Boy chair. [*Laughter*] Nobody could keep us quiet for one moment when we were growing up. Now they are sitting there and behaving like old people, retired people, when they are young. So, there is enormous activity in the school. Fifty percent of the time goes into music, dance, ecology, theater, literature, a variety of things. Academics is fifty percent of the time.

To run a school like this, it needs a massive investment, and it can never be scaled up. We can probably open another two or three schools at the most. We have an average of one adult managing four-and-a-half students. That means there are no rules in the school, no punishment, but it's happening because of constant involvement. This is not a scalable model, but this is for those people who have achieved something in their lives and want their children to get something better.

I am looking at this school as one that could produce future leaders of this country. One beautiful thing about the school is, because it's adjacent to the Yoga Center, almost every day we have some achiever coming there – maybe an actor, a director, a writer, an industrial success or a business leader, all kinds of people. Every day the children are meeting somebody who is a high-achiever. Their level of thought is somewhere else. I must tell you this. Till I was twenty-two years of age, I had not met anybody whom I could call an influencer or a celebrity. But these kids have seen almost any celebrity in the country and internationally all kinds of academics and achievers. [*Applause*] Every day they are meeting such people, so their aspirations are in a completely different place.

The other school we have, Isha Samskriti… You saw the boys performing Kalari*. This is a school where it's compulsory they

---

* Kalaripayattu. Referring to the performance by Isha Samskriti students before the talk.

must stay with us for twelve years, from the age of six to eighteen. This is a school without any academics. Here, there are only six subjects. Kalari is the mother of all martial arts. We have Yoga in a very serious way, not just as a practice but as a way of life. Classical music, classical dance, Sanskrit language and English language. English language is their passport to the world. We are only focusing on the development of the body and the brain to their fullest, without intent.

I don't like this nonsense where at the age of three, people are asking a young boy or a girl, "What do you want to be?" [*Laughter*] If the child says "doctor", whoa! The family is thrilled! [*Laughter*] So without the intent of "What will I become?", just intense focus on everything that they are doing. Because the essence of everything that we have created as Isha is just this: being devoted to the process. No goal.

We don't want to win a race. Just absolutely devoted to what we are doing right now. This is the essence of everything that's being done. This is the essence of Yoga. This is the essence of the spiritual process. This is the essence of a successful life. If you do not do what you are doing right now, but you are thinking of something else elsewhere, obviously you will only dream of great things. In Yoga, there is a saying: "If you have one eye on the goal, you have only one eye to find your way." It's very inefficient. We have two eyes, and everything we have got is only because of what we are doing right now. This is what we are bringing into these children: no intent.

One guarantee I gave the parents is, "After twelve years, I guarantee there will be no certificate."

They said, "What? What will the children do? How will they go to the university?"

I said, "They may not go to the university. They are made for this universe, not for the university." [*Applause*] This is very exclusive education.

So, there is a mass education, a reasonably exclusive education, and a very exclusive education. You must see these children. They are of another level altogether. Their physical prowess and their mental prowess is unbelievable, because they are using their brain and their body *intensely* without intent. This is not new, this is not an experiment. This is the way the *gurukuls* were run in the past. Nobody told them in the end, "You are going to become this." We may have something in our mind, but the child need not know. The child needs to learn to apply themselves absolutely to whatever they need to do right now.

Education, as I went through it… I am not complaining. It's just that I couldn't gather all my mind and put it into education. Only a small part of my mind was involved. I am sorry. I must share how I remember Saraswati.

Ms Sarasa: Sarasa, Sarasa.

Sadhguru: Sarasa? I won't take that liberty. [*Laughs*] The first day she was walking from Regional College of Education. It was called RCE at that time. It's changed now?

Ms Sarasa: Now R.I.E.

Sadhguru: Okay. So, we knew we were getting a new English teacher. She did not come at the beginning of the term. She came a month or two after the term had started. So we were 10th-C. Actually, many times the headmaster of the time thought of hacking this entire section and throwing us into a lake or something. [*Laughter*] It did not happen, but many times he had the thought. [*Laughs*] So, she was walking in... can I describe?

Ms Sarasa: Yeah. [*Laughter*]

Sadhguru: I was outside with a couple of boys. We just thought, "Okay, who is this new teacher?" Because nobody really wants to come into our class. So, I remember Saraswati walking this way, and in a heavily starched white cotton saree with some *butta**, you know, she walked like a peacock. [*Applause*] Well, we carefully examined her. [*Laughter*] And we discussed, "Where is she coming from? Where has she taught before?"

"No, she just passed and she is coming."

"Oh! This is it. Can she handle us?" Because she was just out of college, and we were the first class that she would be handling. She came into the class, and I am sure she was nervous. As a new teacher wanting to reach out, she walked across the room. And she remembers that I was in the last table. At that time, it was tables and chairs. Is it still so?

Professor Y. Sreekanth (Principal of R.I.E., Mysuru): Now it's benches.

Sadhguru: Oh! Benches. We wanted to do something to disrupt her life. [*Laughter*] So, she was talking to the class and probably wanted to reach out to the last bench and show that she was a concerned teacher. When she came there, she was facing the other side and leaning on my table. So I felt inspired. And I opened my pen and let out the ink on her white, starched saree, which very readily absorbed all of it. And, of course, she did not

---

* Design motif.

notice. And some of those who were giggling then are here and still giggling. [*Laughter*] Then she went. Probably somebody in the staff room would have told her that there is a big patch of ink on her saree. Then, post lunch hour, I was in the classroom. I was called to come to the staff room.

I thought it would be one more suspension. [*Laughter*] Because in those two years, I think I was suspended at least six times. So, I went there, and she asked me for my pen. I gave it to her. I thought she was going to confiscate it as proof of an empty pen. Then she took out an ink bottle, filled my pen, and gave it back to me. I said, "Thank you, ma'am," and went back to the class. And that one thing made me in such a way that I never forgot that one teacher. [*Applause*]

Ms Sarasa: Thank you, Guru-ji. It's been wonderful. Really. Especially the way we have to focus on learning, you have given a lot of input. We'll keep it in mind when we really deal with learners. [*Applause*]

(The next segment conducted by student-moderators is about to begin.)

Sadhguru: Oh, this is a youthful assault on me! [*Laughter*]

Anugraha (Moderator): Namaskaram. I am Anugraha Kurien. I am from Hyderabad, and I am a fourth-year BEd student.

Snehali (Moderator): I am Snehali. I am in third year BA, BEd. I am from Bangalore.

Vedavyasa (Moderator): I am Vedavyasa. I am in second year BSc, BEd. I am from Anantapur district, Andhra Pradesh.

Anugraha: So, let's begin our question–answer session.

Sadhguru: Yes, ma'am. [*Laughter*]

Vedavyasa: First of all, namaskaras to you Sadhguru. Sadhguru, I have worked very hard to secure a first rank in the common entrance examination and get myself placed here. But my brother tells me that it's my destiny that has put me here. Is it really my destiny or my hard work that has placed me here?

Sadhguru: Where is your brother placed, hm? [*Laughter*] See, what people are generally calling "destiny" is essentially what they end up creating unconsciously. When I say "unconsciously", as everybody sits here right now, there is physical activity going on within this system. There is a mental process, emotional activity and, of course, the life energies are active. Every moment they are taking in hundreds of inputs, whether you are conscious or not. So, if I ask you a question – since this morning, from the time you woke up till now, how much of these four dimensions of activity have you conducted consciously? What percentage do you think?

Vedavyasa: Few things.

Sadhguru: How much percentage do you think?

Vedavyasa: Twenty-five percent.

Sadhguru: You are a very generous man! [*Laughter*] It's well below one percent. If you walk from there to there [*gestures across the venue*], there'll be twenty-five different kinds of smells that you are not conscious of, but the body registers and records. There are a hundred different kinds of sounds that the body registers that you are not conscious of. Throughout the day and night, in wakefulness and in sleep, this is happening. When you are only conscious of less than one percent of your activity, when you are doing ninety-nine percent of things unconsciously, definitely life will look like an accident.

See, it so happened that somebody fell off their vehicle on the street and had a brain injury; after that, suddenly, they started working their mathematics in a wonderful way. But that was only one. A thousand other people who cracked their skulls never recovered from it; they died, or lived on much diminished. So, being accidentally fortunate is not the way to exist. Whenever a pleasant accident happens, we say it's destiny. Some of you even say, "God is doing things to me." I don't know, when did you make a partnership with him?

Shall I tell you a story? Are you okay? This happened. Sherlock Holmes and Watson went out camping. Early morning at 3.30 a.m., Sherlock Holmes nudged Watson. Watson opened his eyes and said, "What?"

"What do you see?" Sherlock Holmes asked.

"Well, I see a clear sky and stars."

"What does that mean to you?"

Watson said, "Well, that means tomorrow is going to be a wonderful, sunny day." Then he asked, "What does it mean to *you*?"

Sherlock Holmes said, "It means someone has stolen our tent." [*Laughter*]

So, we don't know what went missing, and something may fall here and there by chance. But that's not the way life works. If a human being doesn't take it upon himself or herself to make their own destiny, well, they are still having an evolutionary problem. That is, they are still not fully there, because being human means we can conduct our life consciously, we can craft our life the way we want. But this destiny business is a good insurance to handle your failure. Whenever you fail – it's destiny, God's will. This has been going on for a long time.

This is not the fundamental nature of this culture. In this culture we taught you right from ancient times, "Your life is your karma." Did we tell you or no? This means your life is your making. Nobody told you there is a god up there who will do things to you. No interstellar influence on you – it's you! There are a million impacts on us, but what we make out of them is still us, isn't it? What is thrown at us is not in our hands, what comes our way is not in our hands, but what we make out of it is one hundred percent in our hands.

I must tell you this: When I first went to Coimbatore and we started setting up the Yoga Center... This country is very strange. Now they are all clapping their hands, but at that time, simply rumors were going around, "Oh! They are doing drugs. They are here to kill the wildlife. They are killing tigers, elephants." All kinds of things. Even media was reporting these kinds of things.

Then a hundred prominent people in the town met and said, "This Yoga is spreading like a disease" – these were the words! – "we have to do something."

Then, some young hothead said, "Let's take a truckload of people and pull down the whole thing." Because the whole Yoga Center at that time was just thatched roof sheds. Today, it is among the most prominent places in the country.

When they said this, there was a wise old man who is no more. He said, "See, you don't know who you're dealing with. I know this man. If you throw stones at him, he will build

something out of those stones. Don't throw stones at him."
[*Applause*]

You cannot decide what comes at you, but you can definitely decide what you make out of it, isn't it? This is where your dint is.

Vedavyasa: Thank you, Sadhguru.

Snehali: Sadhguru, all through school and college, we are taught to give importance to ourselves – self-love, self-confidence, self-esteem.

Sadhguru: What is this self-love? What's happening in your school? [*Laughter*]

Snehali: In society, I mean, in general. They teach us to give importance to ourselves to such an extent that we no longer know how to be humble. So, can you please tell us how we can become humble again?

Sadhguru: Oh! See, there is no need to be humble, nor is there a need to be arrogant. Now that you are asking me this question, let me tell you. My daughter traveled alone in the car with me when she was three-and-a-half months old. I drove all over the country with this little baby in the car. So, she grew up in many people's homes. This is the problem with adults – when they see a child, they pounce on them like predatory animals. They want to teach them something. [*Laughter*] Everybody wants to teach "one, two, three, four" or "A, B, C, D" or "Mary had a little lamb". I said, "See, I don't want her to know 'A B C', 'one, two, three', nor do I care whether Mary had a lamb or not." [*Laughter*] I made one rule: you can play with her, but nobody is going to teach her anything. So she grew up happy. By the time she was eighteen months old, she was fluently speaking three languages. Because nobody taught her anything, she was listening. She was not chanting "Mary had a little lamb", no rhymes, no language, no mathematics – simply life.

I thought I'll never send her to school, but the only reason I did send her was because, you know, her age group is important. So, she went to school. When she was around twelve years of age, she came home one day a little disturbed about what had happened in the school. Then she said, "You are teaching everybody so many things, but you are not teaching me anything."

I said, "See, I am not known to do things unsolicited. Now that you have come, let's see. See, this is all you have to know: never look down on anybody, never look up to anybody." And she looked at me questioningly, as if to say "What about you?". I said, "Not even me."

If you look up to me, probably you will make a picture and nail me to your wall. But you will miss the whole point of who I am. You must look at me as I am. Not looking up. Never look up to anybody, never look down on anybody.

This looks very simple, but try it and see. In your mind you have decided what is good, what is bad, what is high, what is low, what is virtue, what is sin, what is filth, what is wealth. Everything is already determined. Once you have done this, there is no way. What you think is bad, you will look down on; what you think is good, you will look up to. If you remove this and just learn to look at life for what it is, you will effortlessly navigate through your life.

Right now, this is the problem: you are looking up to some people and looking down on some people and trying to be humble with them. There is no need to be humble. Treat everybody as rough as you treat yourself – that is, if you are treating yourself rough. If you are pandering to yourself, try to do the same with others; then you will get tired and treat them rough anyway. [*Laughter*] So this is simple. I am telling you the same thing I told her. It worked miraculously for her. Never look up to anybody, never look down on anybody. Just see everything the way it is.

This is the fundamental of this culture. If you go to the temple, what do you do? Namaskaram. You see a man, what do you do? Namaskaram. You see a woman, what do you do? Namaskaram. You see a tree, what do you do? Namaskaram. You see a rock, what do you do? Namaskaram. A cow, snake, donkey, monkey, everybody – namaskaram.

Fundamentally, this is called *vairagya*. Vairagya does not mean giving up your life and going somewhere. There is nowhere to go. Wherever you go it is still life, isn't it? Literally, "vairagya" means beyond color. That means you've become transparent. If you are transparent, every dimension of life can pass through you but will leave you untouched. You can handle life to the extent you wish. What you can handle you handle; what you cannot handle you don't. The moment you think something is good, something is bad, somebody is high, somebody is low, now many things that you can do in your life, you will not do. It's a brief life. It's a limited amount of time for the human potential to flower. In this life, if you are choosing what to do and what not to do – no. Everything that you can do must happen. What you cannot do, it doesn't happen – it's okay. [*Applause*]

Vedavyasa: Sadhguru, I am a student with a science background. Most of the religions in this world proclaim that God has created human beings, but our evolutionary science is saying that human beings have come from monkeys. Which one should I believe?

Sadhguru: What do you feel closer to? [*Laughter*]

Vedavyasa: Being a human, I think that I have evolved from humans.

Sadhguru: [*Laughs*] See, if you are someone who is on a reverse gear, then you must choose the first one. Your religious people are telling you you came from God because you are going in that direction. Better not to go in the direction of a monkey, go back to God. But if you're planning to evolve, then better go with Darwin. Is there room for evolution for you, or are you super evolved already? I am asking.

Vedavyasa: There is room for evolution.

Sadhguru: If there is room for evolution, that means there is a possibility that you can become a better man than what you are today. So, if you are going in forward gear, go with Darwin. If you are in reverse gear, go with God. [*Laughter*] Yes. Because if you want to go on that path, that needs devotion. Devotion means you want to dissolve into your object of devotion. Whatever it is, you want to dissolve into it. So in a way, it is a way of making yourself less and less, so that you become nothing, literally. It's a wonderful way to live. It does not sound good when you say that you want to become less and less. But when you become really nothing, you also become limitless.

Devotion is one way to go. But you don't have that because you've gone through a little bit of modern education and you're beginning to think logically. Now if you think logically, naturally you can see life has evolved on this planet. There's no question about that. If you want to go forward, you must see just behind you is the monkey. One step backward, and you will be right there. Better you move forward quickly! Some of the scientists are saying today that the DNA difference between you and a chimpanzee is only 1.23 percent. 1.23 percent is not much of a difference, isn't it? But see, just 1.23 percent is a *world* of difference!

If you are not happy with 1.23 percent, you must accelerate your evolution. The entire system of Yoga is just this – in every dimension of who you are, how to hasten your process. Now that you are talking about evolution, a goat could have become a giraffe, but it would take so many million years. A pig could have become an elephant, but it would take so many million years. A monkey became a man, and it happened rather quickly to such an extent that anthropologists are saying there must be a missing link somewhere.

Now, if evolution happened... When you were a monkey, you did not desire to become a human being. Nature just pushed you on. It's not a conscious thing. It's just life's longing to get better. From an amoeba to here, just imagine the volume of work that's been done. Incredible, isn't it? Maybe nobody is clear about the number of years it took. One million years, ten million years, it doesn't matter. With our lifespan, one million years is as good as a hundred million. It doesn't really matter, except for academics. Whatever amount of time it took from a single-celled creature to the human being, a tremendous amount of work has been done! But now you have been rendered in a space where your evolution has to be conscious. Over 15,000 years ago,

Adiyogi said this when his seven disciples asked, "How did life happen?" You have heard of the nine *avatars*? What are they?

Vedavyasa: Matsya, Kurma, Varaha, Vamana, Narasimha, Parashurama, Rama...

Sadhguru: Not bad. He's from Andhra Pradesh...

Vedavyasa: ...Krishna, Buddha, Kalki. [*Cheers*]

Sadhguru: So, please look at what he is saying. This is very much in parallel with what Charles Darwin is saying. First is fish, Matsya Avatara. Next is amphibious [*suited for both land and water*] – turtle. Then, he is skipping all the other small forms and coming to the mammals. The first mammal we are talking about is a boar or a pig. Wild boar hunters and eaters know the hardest animal to kill is always a boar because it's so rooted in the body. Even today if you behave badly, the girls will say, "He is like a pig." [*Laughter*] If something is very crude, you say it's like a pig. So, the first mammal is the pig. What's the next avatara?

Vedavyasa: Vamana.

Sadhguru: No. Narasimha. Narasimha means half-man, half-animal. Next is Vamana which means a dwarfed man. Next is Parashurama, a full-fledged man but explosive, uncontrolled, volatile. So volatile that he lopped off his own mother's head. Next one is Rama, a peaceful man. Next one is Krishna, a loving man, an exuberant man. Next one is Buddha, a meditative man. Next one is supposed to be a mystical man. This is not about those individual people. These people are being used as milestones. This is the nature of development of life. In many ways, this is running parallel to Darwin's theory of evolution.

Darwin's theory of evolution is only about 150 years old. Adiyogi spoke about this over 15,000 years ago. [*Applause*]

And then, naturally, the next question is, "Can we evolve further?" Because right now you find, when you want to study for your examination, you wish you had a little more brain. Hello? Does it happen or no?

Audience: Yes.

Sadhguru: Naturally the question is, "Can I evolve further?" If a single-celled animal can become this much, can I go further? Modern neurologists are saying the very same thing Adiyogi said, but in a different language. I will not go into the elaborate arithmetic of this. The planet Earth, the moon and the sun are very important in the making of the human system. There are another six celestial bodies that are also playing an important role, but the planet, the moon and the sun are the most important. This is why the entire Yogic system is around these three aspects. These three have significant roles, unless something fundamental about the solar system changes. Adiyogi said, "Considering the nature of the solar system, your body cannot evolve further, but you can evolve consciously." When we say we can evolve consciously, we can take you as an experiment if you are willing.

Vedavyasa: Yes.

Sadhguru: We can show you that your very fundamental genetics will change within a matter of three to nine months by doing certain things with your system. If you are willing to give yourself to a certain discipline, your very genetics can be altered. Your level of intelligence can be changed. The way you experience life can be changed. So, he said that you can evolve consciously, but you cannot evolve physically unless something about the planetary system changes. Modern neurologists are saying something very similar. I will not go into the detail because of time, but you can evolve. So, if you are going forward, choose Darwin. If you want to go backwards, backwards is not a bad place. Don't think backwards is a negative thing. No. If you want to dissolve, you go towards God. If you want to evolve, this is one way. These are two different ways of doing the same thing. [*Applause*]

Anugraha: Now we will be having the audience question session.

Sadhguru: Audience are all sleeping, hm? [*Laughter*]

Questioner: Namaste, Sadhguru. I have a question for you. You said that Indians have so much knowledge about everything [*Speaking in Kannada*] *Ivaga Bharata vishwakke Guru anta navu heltivi eshtonkade.* (Now we say in many places that India is the Guru to the world.)

Sadhguru: You're saying that or I'm saying it?

Questioner: [*Speaking in Kannada*] *Iga nivu Adiyogi bagge* explain *maadidralla, Sadhguru?* (Just now you explained about Adiyogi, right, Sadhguru?) That 15,000 years ago we had that knowledge.

[*Speaking in Kannada*] *Hang idmele a* knowledge *asht* great *idmele, nav enakkadanna vapas tarakkagalla? Tandre heg tarbahudu?* (If that is so, if that knowledge is so great, why can't we get it back? And if we can, how can we get it back?)

Sadhguru: See, there is no need to bring back anything. People are always talking in terms of how to revive this, how to revive that. It's not about reviving. If you make human beings live consciously, even now, they will speak the same things the Ramas, Krishnas and Adiyogis have spoken in the past. This is one thing you must understand: this is a godless culture. All the people you worship are people who walked this geography at one time. They went through life just like you, all the trials and tribulations. Much more drama than your life.

If we have to take examples, well, we can take Rama, because even today, he is having real estate problems. After nearly 6000 and odd years, still, he cannot settle his property*. [*Laughter*] This happened right through his life also. At a young age, he rightfully became a king. Due to some political reasons he was sent to the forest. And he has a young wife. She is not a tribal woman; she is a princess, not fit to be in the jungle. Well, in your television serials and movies, you might have seen Rama and Sita dancing, and you think it's some kind of a honeymoon. No, going to the jungle is a punishment.

If you don't know what I am talking about, I have lived in the jungles for weeks surviving by myself. If you stay there for a week or fifteen days and come back home, people won't recognize you. Head to toe, you will be bitten by insects. Especially, if you take the girls, you cannot even recognize them when they come out. [*Laughter*] Going to the jungle was not some kind of a picnic; it was a punishment. And as if that was not enough, Ravana came from Sri Lanka and kidnapped his wife. You know the story.

This was in Ayodhya. After all, he was a king. If one wife goes away, he could have found another local solution. Because it's allowed for the king – he could marry a hundred wives if he

---

* Referring to the Ayodhya dispute.

wanted. But the man loves his wife so much, he walks all the way down – not with an army, just with his brother. [*Applause*] She must have meant so much to him, because there was no GPS location as to tell you where Sri Lanka is. It's 6000 years ago. Then he gets there, builds a Tamil army – Tamil people are here also, I think [*Cheers*] – see, look at them! So he builds an army, crosses over, fights a battle, kills hundreds of people, burns down a beautiful city, then gets his wife back.

Then, after a few months of being together, living as a king, his wife was fully pregnant. In that condition, again some political turmoil happens, and he sends her back into the jungle. This must be understood – he is not getting rid of her; she means a world to him. Not just that, for an emperor, his wife being pregnant is a big deal because of the heir. No sonogram, so he didn't know whether it's a boy or a girl. It happened to be boys. But he sent her to the jungle.

Today, many women's groups are asking me, "Sadhguru, what kind of a man is he? Just because somebody complained, he sent his wife to the jungle. We don't like him."

Then I said, "See, do you want a leader in this country who will put the well-being of the citizens of this nation above the well-being of his own family? Do you want such a leader or no? That's the man he is." [*Applause*] Because it's causing distress to the people, who have their own beliefs about her, he sends her out.

If something truly terrible has to happen in somebody's life knowingly or unknowingly, killing your own children is the worst thing that can happen to you. He fought a battle and nearly killed his own children. Fortunately, it did not happen.

Then Sita dies in the jungle. He never gets to see her, nor does she get to see him.

You call this a successful life? It's a serial disaster, isn't it? But we worship this man – not because he is a super-success, not because he can walk upon water or fly in the sky. Simply because no matter what life threw at him – and the worst things were thrown at him – he never became resentful, angry, hateful, or vengeful. He did everything just to the extent it was necessary, and remained a balanced and free man within himself. It is this freedom that we're bowing down to. [*Applause*] We are not bowing down because he is miraculous. Everything that can go wrong in life went wrong with his life, but still life could not get him. This man is above life.

It is that one quality that we bow down to, because that's the only quality we have valued in this culture. If you have forgotten, I am sure if you have heard your mother and grandmother, there was never a conversation without uttering the words "*mukti*", "*moksha*", "*karma*", "*prarabdha*". The only value in this culture has always been liberation, freedom. Mukti is the goal, not God, not heaven, or the pleasures of heaven. Only liberation. Liberation does not mean you go somewhere. Liberation means you're here doing life in full intensity, but life doesn't leave a single scratch upon you.

Anugraha: Thank you, Sadhguru. Now we will have a social media question.

Vedavyasa: The first question, Sadhguru, is from Brinda. "Will uniform civil code be a possibility in India? I think at least after one or two generations of utilizing the caste-based reservation in education and jobs, the third generation should not be given reservation."

Sadhguru: Well, these are two different things. It's a two-in-one question. Uniform civil code – is it a possibility? Well, we must make it possible. As long as you have a nation where different people have different rules, you will keep people different. If you want to make all of them Indians, there must be one law in the country – there is no other way you can integrate a nation. One law for you, one law for me – definitely we will be two separate people; we will never identify ourselves as one nation. We are continuously facing this problem, but we don't have the courage to fix it. It's time to fix it. [*Applause*]

Reservation is another matter. I know there is a lot of resentment among the young students – "I didn't get the seat; somebody with lesser marks got the seat." But we must understand this: we have treated a whole mass of people in this country for thousands of years like sub-humans. Even today, if you go into the villages, they cannot draw water from the same well, they cannot drink tea from the same cup in a restaurant, they cannot walk through certain streets, they cannot walk in front of a temple, their dead bodies cannot go through the village.

When you treat people like this, if you don't give them some privileges to get back to a level playing field, it will not be fair. At the same time, entry-point reservation should be there, but promotion point definitely has to go. [*Applause*] Both in employment and in education, you give them entry, but do not promote them without the necessary credentials. This has to happen. Otherwise we will sacrifice competence for reservation.

Reservation is an unfortunate situation in the country because we have created a thousand years of discrimination. To level that discrimination, this effort is happening. Have we succeeded in this in the last seventy years? Well, a whole lot of people have moved out of that low-caste trap. Many of them may be sitting here with proper education, holding good positions. It's fantastic to see that. But there is a substantial amount of population still stuck there.

As time goes by, we must calibrate the reservation. For different regions, it may be different. How it is in Tamil Nadu, how it is in Bihar, how it is in Gujarat, is different. We must have the courage to calibrate it at least every five years based on the statistics. How much movement of population has happened from poverty to a reasonable level of well-being, and to what extent has discrimination levelled? Accordingly, reservation should be calibrated. But, it's a political thing. No political leader wants to touch it, because election is a number game. It's just like going to an examination. [*Laughter*] Thank you.

Anugraha: We'll be winding up the session. Thank you so much, Sadhguru, for enlightening us.

Sadhguru: Thank you very much.

Anugraha: I request Professor Y. Sreekanth…

Professor Y. Sreekanth: A small felicitation to you, sir. A token of gratitude for being here at R.I.E., Mysore.

Sadhguru: The gratitude is not from your side. I've been in thousands and thousands of events all over the world, but this means a lot to me. [*Applause*]

(Professor Y. Sreekanth gives Sadhguru a record of his admission register to the school as a memento)

Sadhguru: [*Laughs*] I'm glad you didn't get the marks card. [*Laughter*]

Professor Y. Sreekanth: [*Laughs*] It's not a marks card.

Sadhguru: [*Laughs*] Okay. Thank you. [*Holding up the memento*] See, I *did* go to school! [*Laughter*]

AN OPPORTUNITY OF A LIFETIME

On the cool, breezy evening of 15 September, Anugraha was waiting in her school's quadrangle with bated breath for the guest she was slated to interview – the first in her schooling career. "Soon, Sadhguru drove in, and the crowd erupted in joy. He came out of the car with a swag that would embarrass the coolest dudes on the campus," she quips. "I had this beautiful sensation enveloping my entire body when I saw Sadhguru for the first time," she adds. "I couldn't believe that I was one of the three students who would have the opportunity to share the stage with Sadhguru."

Vedavyasa, another moderator, shared her sentiment. "I was loitering around the event venue for a few days thinking of how I could help out," he says. As he was neatly arranging chairs, he was totally unaware of what would soon come his way. To his utter amazement, he was given a wild-card entry onto the stage just two days before the event. "It was sheer serendipity! Actually, I was not the chosen one. One of the selected moderators offered me their seat, and I immediately grasped the opportunity."

A CITY WELCOMES ITS SON

Meanwhile, Aravind, then a senior student at Demonstration Multipurpose School (DMS), Mysuru, was busy behind the scenes. Many years ago, Aravind's family had undergone the Isha Yoga program (now known as Inner Engineering) designed by Sadhguru. But Aravind wasn't drawn to "Gurus", and Sadhguru was no exception. Yet, ten years later, he was among the most excited of the 600 students in the campus. The school management had appointed him as a coordinator for the event. His responsibilities entailed managing a team of sixty student-volunteers, setting up the venue to receive the school's most influential alumnus, ensuring the event was well-publicized, pooling questions from students, alumni and social media, besides troubleshooting and other unstated responsibilities.

Preparations had begun weeks before the event, and as the day inched closer, "We could just feel a different energy in the air. Never before had I seen the students and teachers so excited," shares Aravind. The fever of anticipation even caught the people of Mysuru. It was as if the whole city was coming alive to receive its own boy who was returning after many years, now as a world-renowned spiritual master. What had started as a college event was slowly growing into a massive public event. The scale of activities grew by several folds.

For most students and volunteers, it was their first experience of organizing such a big event in Mysuru, and they scrambled until the last minute to get everything in place. On the day of the event, unexpected challenges presented themselves. The overflowing crowd in the event hall meant a sudden demand for more audio devices. Just hours before the talk, they managed to get the equipment only to find that they were missing adaptors! Aravind shares, "I lent the technical team three of mine. After the event, I didn't receive them back, and thought I had lost them for good. But three days later, I felt grateful when the adapters arrived – neatly packed and couriered to me."

MEETING SADHGURU

Behind the stage in the green room, not knowing how to begin a conversation with a mystic, Anugraha introduced herself to Sadhguru and bowed down to seek his blessings. "He said, 'You are a blessing yourself,' referring to the meaning of my name," Anugraha fondly recalls.

"I was very nervous about going on stage and posing questions to Sadhguru. When I introduced myself, Sadhguru said, 'How can I answer questions from Veda

Vyasa, the author of Mahabharata? Please ask me simple questions,' and I burst out laughing," Vedavyasa cites an example of Sadhguru's inimitable way of making one feel at ease. Despite time constraints, he did manage to pose all his questions to Sadhguru without much hesitation. "We categorized the questions under several themes and selected the most popular ones from the lot. By then, we had watched all the previous *Youth and Truth* interactions on YouTube to ensure that we don't repeat the questions asked in previous events."

Today, Vedavyasa is among the most popular alumni of his batch, as videos of his interaction with Sadhguru went viral soon after. He divulges, "My friends and family think I'm a YouTube star."

AN OVERWHELMING RESPONSE

"Honestly, I felt that the students will attend the event for the free *Youth and Truth* T-shirts. But after listening to Sadhguru, they completely forgot about freebies and got fully engrossed in the conversation. His presence left everyone in a kind of a trance," Aravind reveals.

"More than the kind of questions that were asked, it's the way Sadhguru answered them and the way he was able to hold our attention which created maximum impact. For instance, while talking about 'being conscious', neither did he give us any philosophy nor did he quote from the scriptures. Above all, he wasn't preaching," Vedavyasa observes.

This encounter with Sadhguru was something that the students would never forget. "There is this simplicity in Sadhguru though he is revered by millions as their Guru. I feel blessed that I got this opportunity to be in his presence," Anugraha shares.

Vedavyasa was left inspired: "After this event, I feel I must go to Isha Yoga Center in Coimbatore and learn more about the activities there. I'm hoping to get to meet Sadhguru again."

INDIAN INSTITUTE OF TECHNOLOGY, BOMBAY

20 September 2018

Syed (Moderator): Good evening, everybody! I welcome you all to the *Youth and Truth* program at IIT Bombay. My name is Syed Saqlain. I am a PhD student, first year Chemical Engineering. Sadhguru, let me just say, we are honored and blessed to have you here in our presence. [*Applause*]

Sadhguru: It's a privilege for an uneducated man to be in an educational institution… [*Laughs*] [*Applause*] I didn't go there at the right time, so now I'm coming. [*Laughter*]

Syed: So, yeah, without further ado I would like to commence this conversation with your permission.

Sadhguru: Mmhmm, please.

Syed: Yes. So, very often in life we are at crossroads where we are compelled to choose between two options which are equally pleasing. For instance, I just graduated with my BTech this year and I had a few options. I had the option to do MS in Cornell and Johns Hopkins University abroad, or to do a PhD here at IIT Bombay. My heart was leading me towards the US lifestyle, but my brain told me that a PhD at IIT Bombay is the right thing for my career. And evidently, I'm here, but every night when I go to sleep, I wonder about how my life in the US would have been. So, when I am at such a stage, could you tell me what exactly this conflict is, and what I should be doing?

Sadhguru: [*Laughs*] See, we must understand this. When it comes to education, career, choice of partners, marriage, at various points in life people are always thinking what is the best thing to do. Let me tell you – there is no best thing to do in the world. [*Laughter*] Really. Even if you take a very simple thing and throw yourself into it, it could become a great thing. Is it the best thing? No. Because how do you decide what is best? Is what I am doing best or what you are doing best? There is no such thing. Is spiritual process the best thing or chemical engineering the best thing? It'll be foolish even to ask that question, isn't it? So you'll waste your life always wondering what's the best thing.

There is no best thing. Whatever we put our heart and soul into, and do – it may be a simple thing in somebody else's eyes – is a great thing in our experience, and that's what we should do. [*Applause*]

Hiya (Moderator): Hello, everybody. Namaskaram, Sadhguru! My name is Hiya and I am a first-year student here studying in the Aerospace Department. Being college students, we live in dorms and hostels, and we are surrounded by people day in and day out. And with people come opinions and ideas. For instance, let's say I got up in the morning, got ready for class, and am about to leave. One of my friends joins me and she casually comments, "Your hair doesn't look very good today. What's wrong with it?" So, some of us are of the type that we'll rush back to our rooms and just fix it somehow. That might even mean that we are late for class. Let's say I didn't do that, but that thing would keep going on in my mind. I would be in the class thinking about my hair throughout. [*Laughs*] So, others' opinions and ideas have a very deep effect. The amount of effect it has varies from person to person. How do we take the good out of it, and still not lose our individuality and uniqueness in the process?

Sadhguru: [*Laughs*] Now, in this world, probably ten times or even a hundred times more money is being spent on hair products than on brain products. [*Laughter*] It looks like a whole lot of people don't care about what is inside; they only care about what is outside.

For those people who are in a certain stage of their lives where they need to focus on something very intensely, where they need undivided attention to achieve what they want to, normally we shave their heads, you know. So that they don't have to stand in front of the mirror every day. See, I don't have to stand in front of the mirror. Every day I look the same. I don't have to check how I am looking today. When you are focused on something else, certain things get less significance. How we look, is it important? Yes, it is, to some extent. But right now, you are not going to walk the ramp – you are going to class, okay? [*Laughter*] So all you have to do is bundle up your hair, tie it up on top of your head, so that they can't see your hair. They can just see the knot and the amount of hair. That's a good thing. [*Laughs*]

It is not that one should not be concerned about appearance – of course, it matters. But we have to decide where it matters, where it does not matter. If it matters too much everywhere... I have seen people adjusting their hair twenty-seven times in a minute. In your life, if half the time you're adjusting your hair, when the hell are you going to do anything of significance? I am not saying you should not have hair, I am not saying you should not keep it well, but if you are so concerned about your appearance, obviously you're a bit empty inside. If there's some more stuff within you, you wouldn't be *so* concerned about your appearance. Taking care of our appearance to a certain extent is important. Well, if you are going into films or you are a model, you have to take care of it much more, maybe. But for an engineer, if you are presentable, it's fine.

Hiya: And sir, it doesn't end at appearances. It's about general opinions about ourselves, behavioral traits. Like maybe somebody tells me, "You speak very loudly. Why do you do that?" It hasn't happened with me, I am just giving an example. So, how do we take it like a very casual comment?

Sadhguru: I was about to tell you your trousers are torn, but I didn't tell you. [*Laughter*] There was a time when I lived in denims, and nothing but denims, okay? Only Levis. And because of motorcycling and all kinds of things, they would get torn. We had to get them from the United States; they were not available locally in the sixties. So, we used to patch them up. But now people are tearing them up and then wearing them. [*Laughter*] Obviously the message is, you don't care a hoot about what other people think of you. Let that come into every aspect of your life, that you don't really care what other people say about it. [*Applause*] The idea of tearing up new pants and walking around is you don't really care. But that's not the truth with a whole lot of people. "How is it torn? Your pant is torn better than mine!" [*Laughter*]

We've gotten into this mess, essentially because we have not delved into what this one is. There is no profound experience of yourself. Who you are is a bundle of opinions that other people have given. If ten people say you are good, you will become very good. It's like you went outside and somebody told you, "Oh, you are the most wonderful person on this planet." Then you are floating on cloud number what?

Hiya: Nine.

Sadhguru: Only nine? In Tamil Nadu, we do eleven. [*Laughter*] So you are floating on cloud number whatever, and you came home. They told you who you really are, and suddenly, the cloud crashes. Floating on a cloud is not a wise thing to do – you're bound to crash, isn't it?

Gaganpreet (Moderator): Good evening, man of century! I am Gaganpreet Singh pursuing Masters in Geoinformatics and Remote Sensing in CSRE Department at IIT Bombay, sir. Sadhguru, I belong to the land of five rivers. And now, wherever I go there, I see all the able people dream of going to the land of the maple leaf, that we call Canada. [*Laughter*] And when I interact with them, they have one motive – we'll go there, we will earn in dollars and send it back, adopt one of the villages, build roads, hospital and schools. What is the harm in it?

Then, I see soldiers, farmers, social activists, teachers who are working at the grassroots level. So, in IIT, we will get a good opportunity to go abroad and earn Canadian dollars, or we can work here. But whatever we can contribute as tax is quite minuscule compared to the funding we get from abroad. Which route should I take?

Sadhguru: Oh! [*Laughs*] See, India is an ancient culture. This means there are many benefits because there is immense wisdom, and there is also a heap of bullshit! [*Laughter*] To sift through this bull and get to the wisdom takes us some effort.

The five rivers are in a pathetic state. And the land has been ripped through completely. So, naturally, people want to go elsewhere and do the same to another continent. Well, Punjab was an important part of the Green Revolution in this country; that's very wonderful. But at the same time, this Green Revolution became relevant in our country simply because we were in a desperate state. We had bad famines every three to four years in the last century where millions of people died. But the last famine we have had was probably in the 1960s. After that we have had droughts, bad agricultural years, but no famines – at least no mass deaths. So it's fantastic. These were desperate measures that we took to beat that situation. We exploited the land in a certain way that is not healthy in the long term. We did it because it was a kind of emergency for the nation.

Now, should I go abroad and send Canadian dollars? I am not saying you should not go abroad. If you think you're going to learn something better there, acquire some more skills than what you can gather here, if there are possibilities there in terms of profession or even if you are going to work there, it's fine.

But don't think in terms of earning dollars, and then coming back and building your village. That's a long shot! Actually, what we need in this country is not necessarily dollars. What we need is corruption-free, clear, focused and dedicated people. That's what we are missing. [*Applause*]

Money is there. We don't really need money from outside. It is just that we are constantly busy working against each other at so many levels. Our energies are simply spent throwing things at each other all the time. If you don't understand what I am saying, just turn on one of the English news channels in the evening and watch *how* much energy is wasted simply saying rubbish against each other, endlessly. [*Applause*] And slowly, we are losing all sense of civilization in this argument. We think we are debating; no, we are just shouting abuses at each other. A debate means to explore – to use two brains instead of one to explore something. Simply throwing things at each other is not debate. We might as well throw stones at each other, instead of hurling abuses. At least it'll end soon. [*Laughter*]

So, immense waste of energy, and no cleanliness. When I say "no cleanliness", I mean a whole lot of people are simply innocent of integrity. They're not corrupt; they're just innocent of integrity. They don't know what it is. Because we are a nation that is not controlled by any moral code. Nobody told us, "Thou shall not do this or that." But in this culture, we managed ourselves by constantly stirring up human consciousness in every generation. Well, you also come from the land of Gurus, because the idea is to stir up human consciousness rather than give you a set of morals to follow. Morals can be subverted by anybody, but when it arises within you, it's a natural expression of who you are.

This has been the process, but over a period of time, because of invasions and occupations, these systems of transmitting consciousness or invigorating human consciousness have largely collapsed. Today, anybody can read half a book that is considered sacred, become a guru and do whatever they want. You have a lot of them in the land of five rivers. Because this system has collapsed, people have not invested their life into knowing something. They're just reading half a book and trying to preach. As technology develops in the next ten to fifteen years, reading a textbook and telling people what it is all about will become irrelevant in schools and colleges. Similarly, reading scriptures and telling people what they're about has already become pretty irrelevant, because everybody can read and, most probably, understand better than the preacher.

There is so much to be done here if you have integrity. I am focusing on integrity because this has been a scarce thing. I must tell you this. About seven or eight years ago, I was in the United States and somebody told me, "Sadhguru, every day over 100,000 people are typing the word 'spiritual' on the net."

I said, "Is that so?" Because I never typed that word. I said, "Type it, let's see what comes."

On Google, if you type "spiritual", the first thing that comes up is a spà in Mexico. [*Laughter*] Second thing that comes up is a call-girl in northern California. She has spiritual sex, spiritual whatever. She knows SEO, you know? She's used "spiritual" in twenty-five different places in her website, so if you type "spiritual", she comes up.

Then, I thought this was a shame. For thousands of years, for anything spiritual, people looked to the East, towards India. So, I said, "Let's open a platform as India being the spiritual gateway to the world." Everybody can put their official page, whatever spiritual nonsense they have, on one platform. If they want to put more, they'll have to pay, but one page is free for everybody. If the world types out "spiritual", this big site will come and every form of spirituality is there. People can choose where they want to go. And we thought we will bring some kind of a standard of "three things you must do, three things you must not do" when people from outside the country come to you. I had never met any spiritual leader in the country, never seen them, shared platforms with them, nor had I visited their ashrams. I never had time for those things as I was just busy with what I was doing. For the first time, I made an attempt to meet a lot of people.

Well, I met many absolutely wonderful people who are doing great work, but it was also amazing to see that a whole lot of them are completely innocent of integrity. They just don't know what it is. [*Laughter*] Really, it's incredible! If I walk into an airport or a golf course, I meet men who don't know anything about spirituality, but they are better men. [*Laughs*] Just to give you an example: I was walking in this ashram of somebody who is a big man. As an organization, they are way bigger than us. So, I am walking with them, and I see some nice trees in the ashram. Then I say, "You really have some nice, big trees."

Without looking at the trees, he said, "Ah... ha, ha, that's our *Panchavati*."

---

* Literally "five trees".

I looked and there were only four trees. [*Laughter*] Then I said, "But there are only four trees there."

He said, "Huh, huh, four, five, huh…" He was just surprised that I am actually counting four. When he says five, it's five. Four and five is all *maya*, you know. There is only zero and the infinite; in between all is maya. [*Laughter*]

Whether it is politics or any profession, including spirituality, unfortunately one ingredient that is really weak in India right now is integrity. If you think you have integrity, please stay in India. We don't want one more to escape. [*Applause*]

Gaganpreet: I will, sir.

Syed: Sadhguru, I spend ridiculous amounts of time on my phone. It helps me with my notes, and it keeps me updated with my calendar and connected with the entire world. But the more we depend on it, the more it replaces our menial tasks. Now, technological advances are so steep and rapid that it is predicted that one day, humanity will pass through a time period called "singularity". It is that time period when machines will be intelligent enough to devise machines which are more intelligent than them. And this will happen recursively. So my question here is, do you think these technological advances which are happening will ultimately cause mankind's doom?

Sadhguru: Not necessarily. See, you must understand… A hundred years ago how many things we had to do with our body, and today how many things we have to do with our body, has come down at least 10,000 percent. What do you think? Because everything had to be done using human muscle. Now, if you press a switch, everything will happen. You have seen in all those period movies, two guys will be standing next to a Maharaja and doing the fan. Every time something new came, people who were doing that *punkah* (fan) job felt threatened that their jobs will go away. Of course, they've found something else. Now, nobody is doing punkah anymore. Like this, you don't have to worry. You will find something else to do.

It is uncanny that you asked this question because in the last one year I've been invited to various international conferences to speak about artificial intelligence. I said, "Why me? I am a natural intelligence. [*Laughter*] Why are you calling me to speak about artificial intelligence?" I'm talking about top level people, scientists and others. They're calling it AI, we think Air India. [*Laughter*] Their whole thing is, "If this AI unfolds, we will all lose our jobs." I said, "How fantastic. Find an AI like that for me, so that I'll lose my job and I'll just live." [*Laughs*]

Isn't it fantastic if all of us lose our jobs and we are on a holiday for the rest of our lives? Everything we have to do, if a machine does it, isn't it great that human beings can use their intelligence and time for creating something else altogether, rather than doing menial jobs on a daily basis? If I ask you to hold a punkah for me because the fan is not working, is it not a waste of your intelligence?

Syed: Yes.

Sadhguru: When artificial intelligence comes and does all the things that we want to do, when we are no more concerned about earning a living, I think human genius will unfold. It's a tremendous possibility. Of course, fools who don't know what to do with themselves will bum around, get drunk, get drugged, and lie here and there. But a whole lot of humanity will come to terms with it and fire up in a different way. I think it's great times. We don't really have to worry about your phone. Can I tell you a joke, you're okay?

Syed: Yes, yes, go ahead.

Sadhguru: Because you look serious… [*Laughter*]

A man came into the office with half his face burnt. His boss asked, "What happened to you? Why is your face burnt up like this?"

"No, no, I just attended a call."

He said, "What? You taking a telephone call will burn your face like this?"

"No, I was ironing my clothes. Phone rang, and *shwik* [*gestures holding the iron like a phone on one side of the face*]. [*Laughter*]

Technology is a tremendous enabler. I remember the time when I was building the Isha Foundation. Once in a fortnight or so, I had a telephone-call day. When I stop somewhere on the highway – you've seen that blue-colored metal box with "STD, local, international" and whatever written on it. I would get into those things and start making hundreds of calls. But today, if I just tell my phone, it calls. Oh, I am glad technology is advancing. Life is becoming so much easier and better. But some people don't know how to use it. They are always stuck to it. So many people are getting killed using the phones.

The problem is not of technology. The problem is of compulsiveness. It is unfortunate that there are still so many people dying because of malnourishment. We have the highest malnourished population in the world. But more people on this planet die because they don't know when to stop eating.

Yes, compulsiveness. Food is not the problem, isn't it? Food is good for us. But if you start eating and you don't know when to stop eating, then it becomes a serious problem. The same goes for the phone – you start using it, but you don't know when to stop. Fundamentally we are living an unconscious life, a compulsive life. When you live compulsively, then everything is a problem. There's no one specific thing which is a problem. All the wonderful things that come our way become serious problems in our life simply because we do it compulsively. [*Applause*]

Hiya: Sir, in the Indian society when something goes wrong – let's say, someone is not well – there are three types of people: ones who go to the hospital; ones who rush to the temples; and ones who rush to the astrologers. So we are actually taught from the beginning that inanimate objects and things around us have the power to control our lives. For example, two to three years back, my mother told me to wear a ring which had a gemstone. I still have it on, of course, because that's what mom has said.

Sadhguru: You need to take it off; otherwise the boys will think… [*Laughter*] For good luck you keep it in the pocket. If it's on your finger, they will think…

Hiya: So, that's another issue… [*Laughter*] Other than that, I really do not understand how an inanimate object can control so much in my life or in anybody else's. Can it really do that?

Sadhguru: See, for all the animals, nature has fixed a clear-cut path for what they can do, what they cannot do. That's why they look so sure and certain, and they are peaceful. Once their stomach is full, they are all peaceful. Do you see this? But human beings are being taught that peace is the ultimate goal of life. A buffalo, full stomach, sits peacefully. And for you that is the ultimate goal – what a shame! [*Laughter*] You hold as the ultimate goal what a buffalo can do with a stomach full of grass or whatever else he eats – is it not a shame? But it is being taught as if peace is the ultimate goal of your life.

Coming to fundamentals, if you are not peaceful today, can you enjoy your dinner today? No. Can you just enjoy walking down the street? Can you enjoy the company of a few people around you? No. If not ecstatic, at least you must be peaceful to enjoy anything in your life. So, I'm asking, should it be the first step in your life or the last step in your life? Such people will only rest in peace. [*Laughter*]

Now, do other things have influence on us, particularly inanimate objects? The gems, diamonds, and also the planets? The nature of the planet has a certain influence on the life upon it. You will see on full moon days and new moon days many animals behave in certain specific ways simply because they are influenced by it. You know the whole ocean is rising? When the ocean, which is millions and millions of tons of water, is able to rise, do you think the seventy-two percent of your body that is water won't rise at all? It does.

I don't know if you are conscious of it, but in India most people are. Not only in India, anywhere. Wherever there are mental asylums, they are conscious of it – on full moon days and new moon days, people get exaggerated levels of disturbance in their minds. So people think the new moon and full moon will cause madness. No, that's not the truth. If you are very loving, on a full moon day you will become more loving. If you are very joyful, on a full moon day you will become more joyful. If you are a little crazy, you will get a little more crazy. Whatever is your quality, it gets a little hyped up on that day.

Those who are romantic want a full moon day. Those who want to meditate want full moon day. Those who are a little mad don't want a full moon day. [*Laughter*] Essentially, it's hyping things up a little bit. Of course, today there is another kind of textbook science going on that doesn't observe anything except what happens in the laboratory. These people go on saying that it's all rubbish. No. If you simply pay sufficient attention to your own body, without looking up, without looking at the calendar, you will know when is full moon day and new moon day by yourself. Because it's visible in your system; there is a certain behavior.

Any possibility, if you do not explore it, looks like a problem in your eyes. What is a problem is always a possibility, isn't it?

Audience: Yes.

Sadhguru: So, do inanimate things have impact on you? Yes, if you allow it. Because who you are is not determined by nature; it is left open for you. Every other creature has to live by the laws of nature. You are the only creature on this planet who's been given the freedom to shape your own life. Is it a small thing? This is a product of millions of years of evolution. After these millions of life forms, here we are. We can shape our own lives. You must be moving towards higher and higher levels of freedom on a daily basis. Otherwise, your life is not worth it, because you are getting entangled with the process of life. Even if you go to heaven, it's an entanglement.

Before you joined IIT, when you were writing your entrance tests, the only thing was somehow "I want to get in, I want to get in" – because it's like entering heaven. So it was like "No matter what, I want to get in. That's the only thing I want." After you get in, see how many problems! [*Laughter*] I am asking you a simple question: being on this planet, do you have any proof that you are not already in heaven and making a mess out of it? [*Applause*] Suppose, you took off from this solar system and looked down at it – these fourteen planets and satellites and the works – doesn't planet Earth definitely look like a heavenly body among all these?

Audience: Yes.

Sadhguru: So you are already in heaven and making a mess out of it. And now you want to go to another heaven. Yes, like he wants to go to Canada. [*Applause*] This culture does not value heaven, does not value God; it values only freedom. We want to be even free from the creation and the creator. Mukti, moksha is the ultimate value. [*Applause*] This is not a philosophical value or a religious value; this is something every life is longing for. Only thing is, most human beings are short-sighted and long for it in installments.

See, if people have nothing, they will say, "If I get hundred rupees per day, Shiva, that's all I want." That's a prayer. Hundred rupees fell. For three days, hundred rupees fell – fine, fine, fine. Then on the fourth day: "Only hundred rupees, Shiva? [*Laughter*] What's the problem with you? Are you so stingy? At least 1000 rupees a day." Okay, 1000-rupee note fell. Is the 1000-rupee note in legal tender?

Moderators: Not anymore.

Sadhguru: No, okay, 2000 rupees fell. I don't want to get into trouble with that – "Where is 1000 rupees falling for Sadhguru? Where does he have it?" [*Laughter*] No, no, you asked for 1000 and 2000 fell – "Wonderful, Shiva, fantastic!" After ten days, "Only 2000 rupees?" [*Laughter*] It doesn't matter how much falls, you want something more and something more, isn't it? People think it's about money. This is not about money. People think it's about wealth, power, pleasure, love, knowledge. No, these are all different currencies. Essentially, if we keep you in the same place for too long, you feel suffocated and are looking for expansion, you want to be something more all the time. Yes or no?

Audience: Yes.

Sadhguru: So, there is something within a human being which wants to expand limitlessly. That means it wants to be free, nothing else.

Gaganpreet: Sadhguru, I can proudly say that I am in the top institute of eminence which we now call heaven. [*Sadhguru laughs*] And every student who has come here has burnt himself inside-out to come to this place, and that can be said about each and every institute in India. And, after coming to this heaven also, our days and nights are the same – working very hard to achieve this so-called aim. But still, our careers are not assured. And we don't know whether we will ever achieve the luxurious life of our dreams. Now, seeing the politicians and rich criminals, most of them are not more than fifth pass, but they and their dependents all have an assured career.

Sadhguru: But they don't go to Canada, they go to London. [*Cheers*]

Gaganpreet: Yeah, they go to London. And citizenship of London is assured, and at the same time, they have the best of luxuries. So, my point is, education and working hard day and night for it, is it worth it for this society where we have poorer graduates and richer illiterates?

Sadhguru: Well, we must understand, literacy is on many different levels. ABC is one kind of literacy. On the street, there is another kind of literacy. In the political sphere, another kind of literacy. In the business world, another kind of literacy. So, literacy is not just ABCD. That's a very simplistic way of looking at it. Somebody may not know ABC, but he is very literate with something else.

And above all, you come to an Indian Institute of Technology not for a luxurious life but because of a thirst for knowledge – to know, to become competent, and to be able to create something. [*Applause*] To be able to create something in the world which has not been done until now – not to somehow amass something at somebody's cost and live somewhere where you think it's luxurious. Look at their faces. Well, they look like they've been fed like pigs. That you can see, but do they look joyful, do they look fulfilled, is there some great energy about them? Do you want to live a life like that? Please don't ever seek a life like that.

Mortality is one thing that we've forgotten, that is why we are thinking of all these funny things. Life is just going away. If this sinks into you, that actually minute by minute you are closer to your grave and it's going to be over, what will be the most important thing? How profound your experience of life is. And when it comes to activity, how profoundly can you touch life around you. This is all that matters, isn't it? That when you sit here, in your experience, this is the most profound experience. With intensity and profoundness of your experience, when it comes to activity, what a difference you can make! You may not be thinking like that right now, but think through this. Suppose you cooked something – do you ever?

Gaganpreet: Maggi. [*Laughter*]

Sadhguru: Ohh. He's an MSG or something, hmm. [*Applause*] No, no, no! Not *that* MSG [*referring to the film*]. [*Laughter*] I meant to say… what is that chemical?

Syed: Monosodium Glutamate.

Sadhguru: Yeah. So, if you cook something, even if you make Maggi noodles, and give it to your friend, and he says, "*Bvaack!*" [*gestures puking*] and spits it out, would you like it? If he eats and says, "This is fantastic," then you say, "*Ahh*, nice." Because for even that two-minute job… it's two minutes, right? The ad says two minutes, I don't know how long it takes.

Hiya: That's a myth. It's not two minutes.

Sadhguru: Even for that two-minute job, you want to touch somebody's life. If that guy spat it out, that's the last time you are going to give him those noodles. That saves his life, that's another matter. [*Laughter*]

Let's say you built up a hall, and people look at this and say, "Oh, my God. Terrible!" and nobody wants to come there. Do you want to build such a hall? No, you want people to come and say, "Wow!" You want to write a book nobody reads? No. You want to make a movie that nobody wants to see? No. You want people to see it and walk out with tears in their eyes. Yes or no?

You must understand this – human activity is meaningful only if in some way we touch another life. How many lives is the question. You've heard of Richard Bach? As a generation you never read Richard Bach? [*Looking into the audience*] Nobody? Oh! I am surprised. In our generation there was nobody who did not read Richard Bach. Please look him up.

Richard Bach wrote a book called *Illusions*, and another one called *Jonathan Livingston Seagull*. His entire life is all about flying. I was supposed to fly with him a few years ago. But at the age of seventy-six, he was flying a small plane, and he had an accident and broke some sixteen bones in his body. After that he is not flying. So, his entire life was about flight, and all his books are about flight and how flight relates to our life. And in one of the books he writes that of all the joys of flying, the greatest joy is when you see another pilot and you roll your wings, and he responds by rolling his wings. That's the greatest joy. [*Laughs*] [*Applause*]

After living an absolutely adventurous life, *this is* the greatest joy, because touching another life is always like that. Whether it's music or dance or cooking or writing a book or building something, it matters because it touches another life, isn't it? A criminal does not touch other people's lives like that. You have two ways to live – that is, people are joyful because you are here, or people will be joyful because you are gone. [*Laughter*] There are two ways to live. Please, what will you choose?

Gaganpreet: First one.

Sadhguru: [*Laughs*] People are joyful because you are here. Yes, that's good. So, about somebody living better than us – you should not even look at how somebody is living, because it's a bloody brief life, believe me. Before you know what's happening, it'll be gone. You may not think so. Right now, you think you have a lot of time on your hands. But, if you intensely get involved in something, before you know what is happening, life will be gone. Because it's such a brief life!

Have you noticed on a particular day, if you are very intense and joyfully involved in something, twenty-four hours just pass off like a minute? Is it so? Another day you are a little depressed and looking around at everybody; on that day, twenty-four hours feel like an eon. Time is a very relative experience. Only miserable people will have a *loooong* life, because in misery, time stretches itself. But if you are living an intense and exuberant life, poof! It'll be gone. Hundred years will be gone like that [*snaps fingers*]. Shall I bless you with a *loooong* life?

Gaganpreet: No.

Sadhguru: No. Even if you live to be a hundred, it should feel like you lived for two days. And that is how it will be if you focus on creating something worthwhile. But if you are looking at other people – who is wearing better clothes, who is driving a better car, whose house is better than mine – your life is ruined. Because forever, there will be somebody wearing something better than you, driving something better than you, living in a better home than you. Yes or no? Forever you will become enslaved to that nonsense. Don't ever start your life like that.

All of you are being empowered through education. You must think in terms of "What is it that I can create in this life?". [*Applause*]

Syed: The *Youth and Truth* program has such a wide and intense coverage, nationally and internationally, that social media has been buzzing and flooded with questions. We had a difficult job handpicking some of the questions. Sadhguru, with your permission, I'd like to convey the questions to you.

So, one Pradeep asks, "We are often reprimanded for using swear words. It is nowadays used as colloquial slang. What is the big deal with using slang words when I casually use them without intent?"

Sadhguru: This happened. A nice Catholic girl got married. After three days, she called her mother and said, "Momma, I can't be here with this guy. All the time he is using four-letter words."

Then the mother asked, "What kind of four-letter words is he using?"

She said, "He is talking about 'cook', 'wash', 'iron'…" [*Laughter*]

So, what is wrong in using words? We have our own swear words which are very generic to our languages; some are vulgar, some suggest certain intentions, some refer to our families, [*Laughter*] and some are just simply "poking fun at each other" kind. But largely, the swear words in English language that you use today are essentially picked up from America. It's either toilet or bedroom, okay. [*Laughs*]

I must tell you this. This was way back, nearly forty years ago. A guest had come from Australia and I was supposed to take this person around in Mysore. You know, Mysore is a touristy place. There are many places to see, and I was taking this person on my motorcycle. If I ride hard, I hear in my ears, "Shit." Then I think, "What if I brake?" – "Shit." They see something beautiful, "Shit." [*Laughter*] If the food is very spicy, "Oh, shit!"

I was thinking, why is this person chanting "shit" like a mantra the whole day? [*Laughter*] I thought maybe they're constipated and trying to invoke! [*Laughter*] Because, what should be done in the morning, why are you dragging it through the day, you know? Then I observed, if they're getting angry and say "shit", they become a little calm. I thought, "Oh, it's working for them. I should not disturb this," because I don't believe in disturbing anything that's working for anybody. If it's working, let's leave it. [*Applause*]

I just thought through this. See, we have looked at the whole science of uttering sounds in a powerful manner – what it can do to your consciousness, what it can do to your body, what it can do to invigorate your energy, many aspects of this – and then we say, "Shiva." If I make you utter this one sound with the necessary preparation – you don't have to believe in any god or anything – just the sound will blow your brains out. I can show you this.

Then, I thought, "Shiva... Shit... Shiva. Oh, we arrived at it scientifically. They *somehow* got it." [*Applause*] Even in "Shi-va", it is only "Shi" which is the powerful part; "va" is a dampener so that people don't blow up too much. It's for balance. Well, instead of "va", they put "t". [*Laughter*] Usually when they keep saying it too often, the "t" doesn't come. They say "Shi". Even when I say "Shiva", the "va" doesn't really come out, it's just "Shi". So, I thought it's okay. What does it matter?

Then, immediately some people got very agitated. "Sadhguru, are you saying Shiva and shit are same, highest and the lowest?" [*Laughter*]

I said, "See, this high and low is all your business. But as far as your mind is concerned, in case your vocabulary is stored in an alphabetical order, 'Shiva' and 'shit' are right next to each other. You cannot store 'Shiva' here and 'shit' there. You can't separate them." The question is not about what is good, what is bad, what is right, what is wrong; the question is, will it work everywhere? If you keep shitting all over the place, is it going to work for you?

So, it's all right among young people, you are saying "shit, shit" everywhere. But, now in the United States, even the top administrators are uttering these words just like that. In the international community when they utter such words, it's finished in many ways. You know, if you watch some of these American movies, stand-up comedians and stuff, they are making the whole sentence with one word. The whole sentence is just one word repeated in many different ways. And they are eulogizing that.

I am saying, to develop or evolve a complex language took such a long time. It has taken thousands of years for the human mind. One of the most complicated things that we have come up with as civilizations in the world is language. Language is not a small thing. That way, in India, we have 1300 languages. Right here, you are speaking Marathi, somebody is speaking Telugu, somebody is speaking Kannada, somebody is speaking Konkani. And for thousands of years, though you lived side by side, you maintained your literature, they maintained theirs, and they managed. It takes a certain level of genius to develop the language. Now, a language which had hundreds and thousands of words, you want to reduce to one word, and you think it's a forward step. I'm sorry. [*Applause*]

Gaganpreet: Sadhguru, again, my next question is about the four letters. Love is in the air.

Sadhguru: Hey, what's happening out here? [*Laughter*]

Gaganpreet: When people say they are in love, they think they are in unconditional love, but still, in most of the cases, it's not working. It doesn't lead to happiness. So Sadhguru, when is unconditional love truly possible?

Sadhguru: See, your experience of love means you feel a certain sweetness of emotion within yourself. Either by looking at this person or that person – we don't know who stimulates this in you. It doesn't matter who helped you. But essentially it happened within you, isn't it? Did it happen only within you or was it in the air? I'm trying to clear this air. [*Laughter*]

Gaganpreet: Combination of both.

Sadhguru: Really? It was in the air? No. It only happened within you. Maybe what was happening within you was so exuberant, you saw it everywhere. You are in love, and you think the flowers bloom for you, the birds are singing for you, the clouds are moving for you, hm? All right, I don't want to destroy all the romance, okay. [*Laughter*] But essentially, it's happening within you.

It's wonderful that you are experiencing such sweetness of emotion, stimulated by somebody. You are using the other person as a key to open up an experience within you. I am asking you, why are you using a key when there is no lock, when there is no door, when there is no kind of barrier? It is just that you are a push-start machine. You know what's a push-start machine? If you owned an Ambassador car, twenty-five years ago, you always had to park it on a gradient, because in the morning, two people would have to push it.

Moderators: Yes.

Sadhguru: If you park it like this [*gestures facing uphill*], nobody will come. Your family will not come out of the house. If it's like this [*gestures downhill*], somebody will come and push it. Now all the cars are self-start, many of them remote start. What does it mean? Technological upgradation! You are an institute of technology, all right. I am asking, would you like to upgrade your technology so that you are on self-start? If you wake up in the morning, you are overflowing with joy and love and exuberance by yourself – you don't need anybody to stimulate you. Would you like to be a self-start machine?

Gaganpreet: *Ji*, Sadhguru.

Sadhguru: Then, you must come to me. [*Applause*] Whoever is doing the "love in the air" right now, it's fine. You don't have to tell them anything. But it's very important you are a self-start machine. Otherwise, after some time, you'll try to extract happiness from the other person. That is when these love affairs become tedious and horrible. No. Life should be like this – when it comes to joy, love, exuberance of life, you must be the source of this, isn't it? Well, other things are shared in life.

There are two ways to enter into a relationship. One way is because you want to extract something from somebody. Another way is because you want to share something with somebody. If you are out to share, your life will be good. If you are out to extract, when they close the tap, it's going to get terrible and nasty. You have seen people who thought they are absolute lovers – how terrible it becomes for many of them. Not because there's anything wrong with them. Simply because you started off on the wrong footing thinking "This person is the source of my joy." No. Joy or misery, the source is within you. [*Applause*] It's for you to decide. If you are a joyful human being, they will also want to be with you. If you are a misery, they will endure you for some time.

Shall I tell you a joke? Are you okay?

Gaganpreet: Please, Sadhguru.

Sadhguru: On a certain day, Shankaran Pillai… [*Applause*] was walking in a park in the evening. Sunset time, he saw a young, pretty-looking woman sitting on a stone bench. You know the park benches?

Moderators: Yes, Sadhguru.

Sadhguru: He also went and settled down on the same bench. After some time, he moved a little closer. She moved a little away. He allowed a few minutes and again moved a little closer. She moved a little away. Again he moved closer. Now, there was nowhere else for her to go, because she was at the end of the bench. She pushed him away. Then he waited for two minutes, just for the sun to get to the right angle. Then he went down on his knees and he said, "I love you. I love you like I have never loved anybody in my life."

You know, a woman is a fool for love. If it was in the middle of the afternoon, she wouldn't have believed a damn thing. [*Laughter*] The sun was setting, the ambience was right, and she kind of yielded. Nature took over. Things happened between them. Then he looked at his watch. It was eight o'clock in the evening. He got up and said, "I need to go, I need to go."

She said, "Where are you going? You said you love me."

He said, "My wife is waiting – I need to go!" [*Laughter*]

So, for a whole lot of people, "I love you" is like "open sesame". You have needs to fulfil – physical, psychological, financial, social, and we don't know what else – so you use this mantra, and half the time it works. I am saying, it is important you know the joy of being loving, because sweetness of emotion is needed for you if you want to take really big steps in your life. If you do not have the sweetness of love in your heart, if you try to take big steps in the world, particularly in India, you will end up frustrated and go to Canada. [*Laughter*] In Canada, you meet only moose in most of the country, so it's okay. [*Laughs*]

Syed: The audience here has come to listen to you, and they themselves have so many questions. So, now, I would like to open the forum to the audience so they can ask Sadhguru directly. Yeah, we have a questioner here. Can we have a mic there, please?

Aditi: Sadhguru, Namaskaram. I'm Aditi Sarkar. I am a PhD student here in IIT. Sadhguru, every time we have some submission, me and my friends would plan in advance and try to stick to it, but somehow ultimately, we end up finishing it in the very last minute. I used to think, why didn't I start it early? Why couldn't I finish it early? But then I realized that almost everyone around me is doing the same thing and everyone is procrastinating. So, my question is, why do we knowingly procrastinate?

Sadhguru: See, the longing that you had when you wanted to get into the institute – you have not maintained that same level of longing. How badly you wanted to get in, if you maintained the same level of longing, you would prepone everything that you are doing. Slowly you slacken up and other things interest you, and education sinks down a little bit. If you are doing something that you really want to do, will you prepone or postpone?

Audience: Prepone.

Sadhguru: You'll prepone. If love is in the air, will you prepone or postpone?

Gaganpreet: Prepone, surely. [*Laughter*]

Sadhguru: Prepone. [*Laughs*] So, in a way, intellectually, knowledge is really a love affair. If you get involved, it'll become a much bigger love affair than emotional love affairs. If you conduct your education like a love affair, that you're really involved in it, then you will always prepone, not postpone. But, if you finish too early, that means your faculty must set more stringent timelines, because this is the time of your life when you have to learn how to stretch yourself physically, mentally, and in every possible way. Otherwise, life will crack you when you go outside – unless you find a government job for yourself. [*Applause*] Otherwise, anything else you take up, if you do not know how to physically and mentally stretch yourself without breaking, life will break you somewhere.

The time of being youthful is not a leisure time. When you are growing up, when you are young, you should not be thinking about leisure. Unfortunately, this culture has come from the United States – TGIF, "Thank God, it's Friday." So, if you are only going to enjoy weekends and you are going to suffer the weeks, that means you are doing something that you have no love for. I am asking, why the hell are you doing something that you don't care for? If you invested in what truly matters to you, you will always prepone, not postpone. [*Applause*] [*Speaking to the moderators*] You are also TGIF? [*Laughter*]

Gaganpreet: My professors are sitting here, sir…

Lavanya: Namaskaram, Sadhguru. I'm Lavanya. Thank you for coming to our campus today…

Sadhguru: If you can hold the mic like this… you know, you've seen Lady Gaga? [*Laughter*] Like this [*gestures holding the mic close*].

Lavanya: [*Holding the mic closer*] Is that good?

Sadhguru: Yeah.

Lavanya: I'm very excited to have you here with us. My question is, when I was growing up, as a child, both my parents were working, and there were times I felt lonely and very miserable. Although my parents did give their part of comfort to me, there were times I was feeling lonely on the inside. What can we do so our kids do not feel the same way? Thank you.

Sadhguru: Well, in India, this is the first generation where women have stepped out to work professionally. Otherwise, because we were largely an agricultural community, women worked, but in and around the house. And if they went somewhere to the field, they took their children with them. So, like you see ducks and chicken – if the hen goes, behind it the chicks run – children were always running behind women like that. So, she was always doing her work and still managing and tending to them, and there was a certain cohesiveness to that.

But today, women are going to the office, the factory or some other business, so they can't take their children there.

This is the first generation of women who have stepped out. So in the society, we still don't have proper arrangements where children can be tended to. That system, that facility, and that arrangement has simply not happened in the society yet. I hope it happens quickly. It doesn't matter whether it's a biological parent or somebody else, but children need a loving, caring atmosphere. Just putting nourishment into their stomach is not it; they need some tending, attending to. Somebody should smile at them, laugh at them, do something with them, play with them – this is very needed. Otherwise children will grow up a little sick in their heads. There must be a committed person doing this. It's very important for the child. Unfortunately, in this society, we still don't have those arrangements.

Questioner: Hello.

Sadhguru: Where are you, where are you?

Questioner: Here, on your right.

Sadhguru: Okay.

Questioner: Namaskaram, Sadhguru. When a student steps into college, all of a sudden, he or she gets access to a huge amount of pornographic material which was so far off-limits. And, in the process, they enjoy that and, as we said, experience heaven on earth. And we even have nicknames for those people who overdo it; they masturbate. So, how do we know how much of that is good or bad, and can we have the truth about masturbation? [*Applause*]

Sadhguru: Oh, looks like a popular question, hm? [*Laughs*] See, we have a biology. We cannot put it under the carpet; it's there. It's best we address it for what it is. But right now, the problem is certain religious institutions in the world took this attitude that the very biology of the human being is wrong. Because of this, cultures started hiding it under the carpet.

Well, in this culture we never had it, but after the British came and left, we became more prudish than the British. Before that, if you look at our temples, all the outside temple art is pornographic – if that's what you want call it. We don't call it pornographic; we are only talking about the various dimensions of human biology. We don't see it as wrong, but we see it as the periphery of life. If you stay only there, you will stay on the physical dimension forever, you will not explore anything else. So, in the temple, it's always the periphery. You are supposed to look at that and understand it's the periphery of life, and make an attempt to go deeper.

The most important thing is not to glorify it, at the same time not be in denial of it. Once you come as a human being, your biology is not the front end of your life. It is one part of your life, we are not denying it. This cerebral capability came so that your intelligence becomes the front end of your life, and if you become conscious, your consciousness becomes the front end of your life. Biology is the front end of a bull. It's okay for him; that's all he knows. But biology should not be the front end of a human life.

It's like this – a ninety-five-year-old man went for a medical check-up. His doctor did a thorough check-up and said, "Hey, old boy, you're doing great for ninety-five. No problem with you."

Then the old man asked, "Doctor, but what about my sex life?"

Then the doctor looked at him and asked, "Thinking about it or talking about it?" [*Laughter*]

So, at different stages of life, there are times when you only think about it and talk about it, and there are some times you indulge in it. These are passing phases of life. You are the best judge of how much of it is needed for you. At the same time, you did not come here to explore your biology. [*Laughter*] At least, you should have gone for an MSc in biology. You shouldn't be wasting your time in a technological institute exploring biology. Does that mean you don't have biological needs? You have. It's fine, but it must be on the periphery. It should not become the core of your life.

Animal intelligence works for its biology alone. How to get its food, how to get its mate – this is all its entire life is. If human intelligence also functions like that, you are belying the evolutionary process, because you're rolling back the evolutionary scheme of putting your intelligence and consciousness in the front. A creature which was purely biological evolved into a place which has an intelligence of its own beyond its biology. You are seeing how to take the evolutionary process backwards. It's not necessary. This does not mean you do not have a body. Body has its needs; as there is physical hunger, so there is sexuality. You have to address it in some way, but to what extent is your choice.

Questioner: Hello. Namaskaram, Sadhguru.

Sadhguru: Where are you?

Questioner: Here, Sadhguru. Last row, sir. Left side.

Sadhguru: Okay.

Questioner: So, Sadhguru, I've been watching your videos and they've really changed me a lot. I'm a guitar player and I'm doing engineering. I'm in second year. Obviously, my Indian parents want me to have a steady life. So, they sent me to an engineering college to get settled, but they also support me for guitar. But when I'm studying, I think about guitar and all the players and music. And similarly, when I'm playing, I think about other things and even social circles and all. I don't have a steady mind, and I can't focus on one thing even if I try a lot. Even the mobile is a very big distraction, apparently. So, how do I focus on one thing at a time? I fear that if I give too much time to one thing, I might lose or lack in other things.

Sadhguru: See, the nature of human intelligence is such that it can do many things at the same time, as a process. Most people are misunderstanding intelligence as intellect. Intellect is your thought process; thought is just one dimension of your intelligence. Thought is only happening because of the data that you have gathered in your mind. You cannot think about anything for which you have no data. Isn't it so? *Isn't it so?*

Audience: Yes.

Sadhguru: You're getting sleepy?

Audience: No.

Sadhguru: Because usually we put children to sleep at eight. [*Laughter*]

In the Yogic way, we look at human intelligence as sixteen parts. For the sake of understanding, we can see these sixteen parts as four segments: *buddhi*, *ahankara*, *manas* and *chitta*.

Buddhi means the intellect. The intellect is a cutting instrument – it's like a knife, a scalpel. If you want to dissect something, you need a good, sharp intellect. It can be used for certain aspects of life. Unfortunately, we are using it all-pervasively because other dimensions of intelligence have not even been touched. The next dimension of intelligence is called identity, or ahankara. Depending upon what you are identified with, your intellect will function. You say, "I am a woman" – it'll try to protect your gender. You say, "I'm an Indian" – it'll try to protect your nationality. You say you belong to some religion, it'll try to protect that. Whatever is your identity, your intellect is always working to protect that identity.

The third dimension of your mind is referred to as manas. Manas is a silo of memory. Memory is not just what you remember; your entire body is memory. The body absolutely remembers everything. This memory is the basis of your intellect. If we take away the memory or delink the memory from your intellect, your intellect will become without activity. This is one important dimension of Yoga that we understood.

If you want to continue the knife analogy, the intellect is like a knife, and the hand that holds the knife is identity. A knife is useful or dangerous not because of its quality but depending upon the hand which holds it, isn't it? If you are identified one way, this knife will poke you; if you are identified in a different way, this knife can save your life. Every day, the same knife saves lives and, sometimes, takes lives depending upon which hand holds it. So, if you delink the knife, the hand, and the silo of memory, then your intellect will not be rusted with memory – it will shine with sharpness. You will see this when you go to restaurants and maybe in some homes also. Let's say you ask them to cut a mango. They will use the same knife with which they cut onion to cut the mango. You can't keep the mango in your mouth, the sweetness of it is gone.

If the residual impact of whatever the knife has touched is there on it, slowly it will lose its purpose, isn't it? The same goes for your intellect. If the memory sticks to your intellect, after some time it'll become a useless intellect because it becomes highly prejudiced. So, the entire Yogic system is about this – to dissolve your identity and simply sit here so that your intellect will shine like a razor without any intent.

If intensity without intent comes into your intellect, you can do twenty-five things at the same time, just like that [*snaps fingers*], okay? [*Applause*] So, just listening to videos is no good. We can teach you a simple practice. You start the practice of delinking the intellect from the memory at least for a few minutes a day. You will see your intellect becomes super competent. [*Applause*]

Questioner: Namaskar, Sadhguru! I want to ask you, what is logic? Whenever I start thinking, it seems this is logical and that is illogical. But when I do maths there is ambiguity. If it is logical, then why is it not coming through maths? The second question is, how to express myself? How to create words for my feelings to make others understand what is going on inside me?

Sadhguru: Okay. See, whether somebody else understands what's happening within me or not is not the issue. That is their problem. Whether I perceive what's happening within me or not is the main issue. Is what's happening within me clear to me? This is the important thing. If it's clear to me, whether I find words for it or not, it doesn't matter.

About logical and illogical and mathematics... even mathematics is only logical to a certain point. That is why they came up with calculus; it's quite illogical. [*Laughs*] Yes or no? Because we want to explore dimensions of existence which don't all fall into simple logic, we came up with the type of mathematics that we are doing right now, which is not really logically correct but articulates certain aspects of the existence.

Life is absolutely illogical. Material is logical. So only in handling material aspects of life, we have to be perfectly logical. When it comes to other dimensions of life, they are not logical. In fact, the most beautiful aspects of your life are not logical. If you try to logically find an expression for every dimension of your life, you will feel silly. Suppose you fall in love with somebody and you write it in prose, you will look stupid. But when you write it as poetry, suddenly it's beautiful, because poetry allows illogical expression that prose does not.

In every sphere of life, people have understood that logic has its limits and they have found ways to explore life through means that are not necessarily a hundred percent logical. Your logic fits into this life perfectly well, but don't try to fit the life into logic. It doesn't fit. [*Applause*]

Questioner: Namaskar, Sadhguru. Thanks for giving me this opportunity. I want to ask, when we are roaming on the street, even the dog is not happy and we are also not happy...

Sadhguru: Please hold the mic a little closer to you, yeah. It's quite safe. [*Laughter*]

Questioner: Mother Nature gave us a brain. We are responsible for taking care of the plants, birds, everything, but we are not taking care of them. We are not happy ourselves, and we are not keeping Mother Nature happy.

Sadhguru: Okay.

Questioner: Thank you.

Sadhguru: I don't know where you saw an unhappy dog. It must be a Mumbai dog. [*Laughter*] Must be a dog on a Mumbai street where too many vehicles and things are moving around. Poor guy, he's just surviving day-to-day. Otherwise, dogs are really very happy if their stomach is full. Go away to the villages and small towns and see, they're just romping around happily. As long as they are well fed, they are happy. Human beings also; it's not that everybody is unhappy. There are happy people and unhappy people – there always were, still are.

We are seeing how to increase the percentage of happy people so that we can live in a joyful world. It's out of my greed that I am incessantly active in the world, because I want to live in a joyful world. But a lot of people are carrying an end-of-the-world expression on their faces, as if the world is going to end today. Especially, if the world is going to end today, it's time to be joyful, isn't it? So, we are living irresponsibly for sure. We are like this for various reasons. In this country, we have an enormous culture – *enormous*. No nation on the planet has 12,000 to 15,000 years of history and culture. We can use this culture to become wise and wonderful, but a whole lot of people use it in a different way. Because you said everybody is unhappy, I thought I'll tell you a joke. You okay?

Audience: Yes!

Sadhguru: It once happened. The Iraqi ambassador to India met Shankaran Pillai. When people of two ancient cultures meet, it's bullshit time, always! Because we've got nothing much to show in the present, we talk a lot about the past. Well, we are proud about the past history of this nation, the culture of this nation, but you cannot live there; you can only live here. But this is the usual thing to talk about the past.

The Mesopotamian culture was big. So the Iraqi ambassador started off, "Our culture is so great. We have excavated 2500-year-old sites in Iraq, and we found copper wires. It proves that we had telegraph 2500 years ago."

Shankaran Pillai said, "Hah! That is nothing! We have excavated sites which are 5000 to 7000 years old, and we found nothing. That means we had wireless!" [*Laughter*]

Because we are engaged in debates like this, we are not taking care of many immediate things that we need to take care of – how to keep our street clean, our city clean, how to see that everybody is fed well. We are not taking care of this because we are a little in the wireless state. [*Applause*]

Syed: We have a shortage of time, so we'll be stopping here. Sadhguru, we thank you again for being here with us, for sharing your pearls of wisdom, for enlightening us here, and for the *Youth and Truth* program.

Sadhguru: So getting into a coveted place like this – which hundreds of thousands of students want to get into and barely three or four hundred people do – which, even internationally, is recognized as a premier institution… when you are in a place like this, it's my wish and my blessing that you must really acquire knowledge. And knowledge is no good unless it is dispensed with love and compassion in the world. Just pure knowledge without love and compassion, without involvement in life around us, can become a very cruel force. Technology is the best thing that's happened to us and the worst thing that's happened to us, unfortunately. You have to make sure that technology is the best thing that's happened to us in the coming generation. In the previous generation, all of us have used technology in a negative way. Yes, we've made bombs, we've made pollution, we've made terrible things. It's for you to create a wonderful world with the knowledge that you are garnering here. Please make use of this and create something really fabulous for this world. Thank you very much. [*Applause*]

AN ISLET IN THE ISLAND CITY

There was a reason IIT Bombay did not make it to the original list of the twenty-odd institutes that Sadhguru would visit as part of the *Youth and Truth* programs. The idea was for students to pose their questions unhesitatingly, bring out their deepest and most uncomfortable doubts, including many trending and popular questions from social media. Techie, "nerdy" students did not necessarily fit the bill, the core team thought. Yet, given the impressive level of enthusiasm from the students and faculty alike, and for the diversity of representation, IIT Bombay was selected at last.

Located on a 550-acre sprawling green campus in Mumbai's eastern suburb, IIT Bombay is like a private island situated in a city overflowing with people, a hodgepodge of buildings and out-of-control traffic. The technological institute's serene campus with more pedestrians than vehicles has a subtle unwritten order and discipline. While urban nightlife rages outside of campus, street lights of IIT Bombay are turned off at night even as dormitories remain lit. Here, into the wee morning hours, students strive to decode technological mysteries that would solve several of the world's pressing challenges, and in turn their own.

However, a dark flipside haunts the aspirational students. High levels of stress and a few unfortunate student suicides every year have been a cause of concern at IIT-B for some time now. And so, on the first International Day of Yoga, a wellness club "Yogastha" (meaning "established in Yoga") was set up under the students' gymkhana in IIT-B. Since its inception, Yogastha has been working towards a stress-free, peaceful campus community through its fitness and Yoga sessions. "Yogastha had previously invited Sadhguru to address the students at the campus, but it didn't work out due to Sadhguru's schedule. We jumped at this opportunity in 2018 when it came our way," shares Nawaz, a PhD student at IIT-B and a key organizer for the event.

LAST-MINUTE RUSH

Confirmation of Sadhguru's visit triggered a wave of enthusiasm among the faculty, including the Dean of

Students' Affairs, who was acquainted with Sadhguru's involvement in social and environmental causes. But the message wasn't percolating down to the key target group of undergraduate students who constituted a significant chunk of campus residents. So a fortnight before the event, the organizing team decided to take some help.

"It was at this juncture that we thought of roping the Mood Indigo team in," Nawaz tells us. Mood Indigo is Asia's largest college cultural festival and a non-profit organization operated by the students of IIT Bombay. "Once MoodI got involved, with their superb network and outreach, it was a cakewalk," says Dr Parul Shah, a professor on the organizing team. "Soon, Isha volunteers, too, joined hands. Together, we managed to publicize the event on social media in less than a week, which we could not pull off in the last two months!"

LIKE A DURACELL BATTERY – FULLY CHARGED!

As a result of the massive effort by the team, there was an overwhelming participation on the day of the event. "I vividly remember that afternoon. Around 5000 to 6000 people were waiting eagerly outside the full auditorium despite the fact that we arranged a live telecast facility in two additional auditoriums," shares Dr Parul.

"I didn't want to miss the event for anything. Sadhguru never hesitates to answer any question that's asked. These are questions that I dare not ask my parents," admits a student who wished to remain anonymous.

"For those three hours, I was completely absorbed in Sadhguru's words and presence. At the end of the session, I felt like a Duracell Battery, fully charged," shares an Electrical Engineering student.

"Generally, spiritual discourses tire young people, but *Youth and Truth* was different. It sparked a flame of curiosity among the students, compelling them to think not only about what they do, but why they do it. It was also this huge opportunity for us to meet and interact with one of the most brilliant minds of our time," says Govind, a member of the organizing team.

GOSSIPING WITH THE MYSTIC

Following a two-hour conversation with the students, Sadhguru was escorted through the hall's narrow aisle among roaring and cheering students. "We ran to protect him from the mob, but he said, 'Look at these people, do they look like people who would harm me? They have so much love in them,'" Govind narrates.

Sadhguru then drove to a nearby outdoor venue for a conversation with PhD students beneath a tree. "Since the sun had set, we thought Sadhguru would just walk around and soon leave, but we were surprised that he spent over an hour there, answering a range of questions," recounts Nawaz.

Sadhguru also made time for the organizing team. The most profound moments for both Dr Parul and Nawaz were the individual interactions they had with him. Dr Parul candidly describes her encounter: "In the auditorium, Sadhguru was supposed to sit next to the dean before the program, but the dean was delayed, so I accompanied Sadhguru until he arrived. I could not bring myself to sit next to him, so I sat on the floor beside his chair. Sadhguru was talking to me, but I could not even speak; I just nodded along. I had told myself I would ask Sadhguru so many questions if I met him, but sitting there next to his feet was already such a blessing."

On the other hand, Nawaz got his chance to talk to Sadhguru in an elevator sometime after the event. He remembers Sadhguru's penetrating and discerning gaze as he looked at him head to toe. "I had the most auspicious opportunity of offering a *mala* (flower garland). He said 'Shambho' and he wore it. I spoke with him about my PhD and my dreams. At the end of the conversation, he said, 'Namaskaram, let's meet again.' I felt very blessed and so grateful, like this was the prize at the end of it."

"If the youth of the world stands up for raising inclusive consciousness, we can address every problem on the planet."

BANARAS HINDU UNIVERSITY, VARANASI

24 September 2018

Aditi (Moderator): My name is Aditi Upadhyay, and I am an intern from the faculty of Dental Sciences. So I take care of people's smiles. [*Applause*]

Priyanshu (Moderator): I am Priyanshu Singh. I'm a research scholar here at the Department of Political Science.

Saransh (Moderator): Namaskaram Sadhguru, it is great to have you here in our campus. My name is Saransh Chaturvedi.... I would like to thank you all for a tremendous response to the *Youth and Truth* event in BHU. [*Applause*] Outside also, more than five hundred people are sitting, watching this live telecast. They were not able to get a seat inside. Thanks to all of them.

So, getting on to the first question, sir... Sadhguru, when I try to see myself as a youth and as a Bachelor in the university, one feeling that hurts me the most is that of unemployment. In the final year, I am not looking at how many marks I should get in the semester, but that I should get the job – that is the most important thing. And then somehow, I saw you. I saw that your job is also very interesting. [*Laughter*] So the question, sir, is… you play with anacondas, you drive F1 cars, you drive helicopters…

Sadhguru: Hey, no anaconda. That was just a king cobra. [*Laughter*]

Saransh: …you drive everything. I am also afraid of the king cobra, sir.

Sadhguru: Hey, you are saying you are from the town of Shiva. He wore a snake around his neck always and what? [*Applause*]

Saransh: Okay, that is a good point, ultimately. I will check it out. So how should I become like you, a cool dude? [*Cheers*]

Sadhguru: You can apply for the job. [*Laughter*] We will process the application, of course. See, we must understand this, in this country in 1990, only seven percent of India was employed, and ninety-three percent were self-employed – all kinds of small, small businesses because there was really no organized employment. I do not know the exact number now – maybe it's gone to fifteen percent or twenty percent. So still over eighty percent of the people are self-employed. I spoke about employment at IIM Bangalore. These are all people doing MBAs, and they asked about employment. I said, "In a developing country you shouldn't be looking for employment. A developing country means there are still a lot of things to be done." As youth, when there are so many things to be done, instead of looking around and seeing what you can do and how you can make something out of that, you are sitting and waiting for somebody to come and give you employment.

Well, this language of "What is the employment rate in the country" comes from the United States, because there, almost everybody is employed except a small segment of entrepreneurs. So, that's a different nation, this is a different nation. Here, there is no organized employment of that scale. People have to find their way, and they *are* finding their way. The rural population is not employed. It's only the urban youth, who, the moment they get educated, somehow get crippled.

Those who are not educated are finding a way to live, isn't it? Those who never went to the college, university, are all finding a way to make a living. But the moment you get educated, should you be more capable or less capable? You should be more capable. So you should give the employment to them and you should become the employer, yes? Tell me, if you look around in Kashi, aren't there a thousand things on the street that you can take up and make a business out of?

Audience: Yes.

Sadhguru: I am not saying there should be no employment generation. Yes, that needs to happen on one level. But don't ever believe 1.3 billion people can be employed in a factory or an office or some organized sector. It's just not possible. It is just that, in a developing country, every one of us has to see how we can develop this country. If you can't do it by yourself, ten of you should get together and do it. But right now the problem is, ten of you cannot get together, even two people can't get together. First change this. If ten of you students get together, you think you can't start something and run it successfully? You can. But you ten people can't get together, yet you want to go into a company where there are a million people working together. This is unrealistic. [*Applause*]

I am on camera. This is going to be a super unpopular video, I know. [*Laughter*] A whole lot of people are going to scream at me, "Oh, he's this, he's that, he doesn't know what is employment... Oh, become a Guru." [*Laughter*] Well, why don't you try? You can try that also; that is also useful. [*Applause*]

Saransh: I will. Now after this event, I will surely apply for being a mystic. [*Laughter*]

Sadhguru: Oh, apply to be a *mistake*? That you don't have to apply for; anyway it happens. [*Laughter*] There is something called as mystic and a mistake.

Saransh: I am also a mistake. In front of you, there might be certain mistakes, but I am totally into being a mystic, what do you say?

Aditi: Okay, moving on. Sadhguru, like you said, that we need to club together and find newer ways to employ people. Basically, it highlights on us being ambitious. So, I am a very ambitious woman, I think, and I have a whole bucket list...

Sadhguru: You have only thirty-two teeth to attend to – that's not very ambitious.

Aditi: No, but that's not it. Do you think that I am a dentist and that is it? No, there's more to life, and that you have professed in one of your videos. So, yes, I am very ambitious, I have a whole bucket list, things that I want to do and achieve...

Sadhguru: Hey, a bucket list is something that you do after you're seventy. [*Laughter*] Before you kick the bucket.

Aditi: But it's long. I can't wait till I get to seventy. [*Laughter*]

Sadhguru: No. You know how this name "bucket list" came? Dying is considered kicking the bucket. So, a bucket list is something you make just a few years before you die – some things that you have not fulfilled. For a young woman, no bucket list, okay? [*Applause*]

Aditi: Okay, a list full of dreams, I would call it.

Sadhguru: Okay.

Aditi: But for girls in this country, for each dream, there is a price to pay. There is a certain way in which society wants us to be; there are unsaid rules, obviously, like "you behave in a particular manner" or "you keep your heads down", or "don't speak much".

Sadhguru: "Don't speak much" is a good idea. [*Cheers*] It's not a bad advice for anybody.

Saransh: Now you are in Shiva *nagari*. [*Laughter*]

Aditi: This was a serious question. [*Laughs*] Okay. So, to follow my dreams, sometimes I need to break some rules, but I don't want to do it at the cost of dishonoring or disrespecting my parents or my loved ones. I want to know how can I be an obedient daughter while at the same time being an independent woman, who lives her life by her own rules? [*Applause*]

Sadhguru: Oh, okay. See, we want to do something that we want to do, and we want to do it with everybody's approval, and then we don't want to pay any price for it. Life doesn't work like that. When we do something that we really want to do, there is a price attached to it, because the nature of life is like that. If you do a certain thing, there is a price to pay, there is a tax. The level of tax depends on how revolutionary your idea is. [*Applause*]

So, this is very unrealistic that people are always thinking – "I want to do this, that, but my father…" Well, you must be glad he brought you into this world. Beyond that, don't complain. What is your father doing? He is doing what he knows best. Yes or no?

Audience: Yes.

Sadhguru: What he knows best, he's doing. If you believe that you know something better than him, first thing is you must be able to convince him. But if he's not able to grasp it, he will not be convinced. Then, you must see how badly you want to do what you want to do – whether it's worth going beyond his lines. If you decide it *is* so, you do it. But there will be a price. Now you want to say, "I will do what I want, but there should be no price." There is no such life, not here, not anywhere. [*Applause*]

Priyanshu: Sadhguru, what an opportunity it is that we have a Yogi among us in the city of the Adiyogi! [*Sadhguru laughs*] And I relate my question to this. We all know for sure that we'll be benefited from you being here, but do we have some special benefit of being in the city of Lord Shiva? I mean, I do not experience it. Are we being benefited directly or indirectly?

Sadhguru: I will need a few minutes for this, okay?

Priyanshu: Please.

Sadhguru: As all of you probably already know, the word "Kashi" means a tower of light. We use the word "light" for many things in human life, simply because of the nature of our visual apparatus. You have a sense of hearing, sense of smell, sense of taste, sense of touch, and you have a sense of sight. Among all these five things, in the human being, the sense of sight is the most powerful one. How much life you drink through your nostrils, through your taste, through your touch, and through your ears, and how much life you drink through your eyes, is very, very disproportionate.

A dog or any other carnivorous animal runs his life through smell. He finds his food that way, he finds his mate that way, and that's how he finds his way, wherever he wants to go. For him, the sense of smell is dominant. But for a human being, our sense of sight is so dominant that it functions best when there is light. So whenever we see something, we say, "It's light." When we see something new, we say, "A new light has come." No new light has come; we are just seeing better. Because we are seeing better, we refer to that as light.

In that context, this is a tower of light. This means, they built a machine – I am calling this a machine because you are in the university – essentially, it's called a *yantra*. The word "yantra" translates into machine in English. As we built bicycles, motorcycles, microphones, microscopes and various things, we built other kinds of machines which were essentially pure energy machines with a physical foundation to them. Small machines, big machines, all kinds of things were built for specific purposes. This is what you call a deity in this country.

They built this phenomenal machine of Kashi, but the vagaries of time, invasions and ignorance, damaged this machine at various levels. But still, it's a fantastic machine. It's not in its full flow, but it is still great. And will anybody benefit from that, from being under its umbrella? Of course they will, but we must understand this – even if the full moon has come up, if your eyes are closed, maybe your blood will surge up a bit, but you will miss the whole beauty of it. The same goes for everything. Whatever we are not conscious of will not exist for us, even if it's there in a very big presence.

So, are you benefiting from it? Definitely on one level, but are you taking full benefit of it? I don't think so. When I look at people, the way they're moving around... Pilgrims will be coming like this [*gestures namaskar*] with tears in their eyes, but people here are going about their little *dhanda* (affairs) completely insensitive to all that is around. So, you may not benefit fully from it unless you're conscious, because subtler aspects of life, especially, will not come to you unless you consciously become receptive. Unfortunately, people have started referring to Kashi as the Mecca of the Hindus. This is not a Mecca. You're not coming here to seek God's grace or something else. You are coming here because this place represents mukti, or liberation or freedom. [*Applause*]

Aditi: The next question, which was a very common thing for the students, is... I am a suffer-in-silence kind of a person, because I believe that if I show my vulnerable side to the society, they might use it against me. So I carry a shield and go out into the world. Is it okay to show our emotions? Does that make us weak? Or should we carry a shield and maybe suffer within ourselves for some time?

Sadhguru: No, you are asking this question as if suffering is very natural to you. Suffering is not natural to you, I want you to understand. See, there is something called as pain and there is something called as suffering. If I put a pin into your body, there is pain, but whether you suffer that or not is your choice. Many times you don't suffer many things that hurt you. Have you seen this? Let's say you want to climb the mountain, or you want to swim across Ganga – every muscle in the body may pain, but the moment you reach that side with this painful body, you are so joyful. Yes or no?

So pain need not translate into suffering. Pain is a natural process in the body. It's very good for you. If there was no pain in the body, most people would not know how to even preserve their physical bodies. Wherever there is no pain, see what all they've done to it. If there was no pain in your nose, in the name of fashion, you would have cut it in so many ways. If there was no pain at all in your body, you would walk on the street with your intestines in your hands. [*Laughter*] Yes, maybe, on the stomach bag you could put "Gucci" and go around. [*Applause*] Don't tell me you won't do these things. If there's no pain at all, wouldn't you have pulled it out? Come on! It's only the pain which is keeping you back.

If you are walking on the street and a bicycle comes in your way, you step back. Do you believe it's because of humility? Consequence of pain, isn't it? If there was no pain, even if a truck came, you would go as if you are indestructible. A lot of people are going like that in spite of the pain. [*Laughs*] The consequence of pain is the only thing that has allowed you to preserve your own body, isn't it? Unfortunately, most human beings are in that state. So, pain is good for you, because it's keeping you in one piece. Otherwise, you would carry your head in your hand and walk around.

Suffering is something that you do mentally. This is your choice. The same thing, you can either suffer it, not suffer it, or enjoy it. Many people are enjoying many painful things, isn't it? So, you're talking like all the time you're suffering: "Should I show it or not show it?" Whether you show it or you don't show it, it's visible. If you are suffering, is it not visible on your face? You may pretend, but everybody knows. Except for those who did not bother to look at your face, people know that you are suffering, isn't it so? They may just keep quiet because they don't want to intrude into your private suffering. Suffering is always a private hell, it's never public, because it happens within you.

So why are we making ourselves into such a mess? Most people after thirty, forty, fifty, sixty years of living here, still have not figured out how to handle their thought and emotion. How unfortunate! When are they going to learn? After a thousand years? People are pretending as if they have a 10,000-year lifespan. At fifty, if you don't know how to handle your thought and emotion, when are you going to learn? I'm asking. This is the most sophisticated machine on the planet. Have you read the user's manual? No. That's all the problem is – not suffering.

Priyanshu: Sadhguru, last year, in the month of September, there was a very big student movement* – particularly the girls came out, demanding for some of their rights. And nowadays, in the last few years, we have seen a number of movements happening in different universities and colleges. Do you think

---

* In reference to a protest demanding safety for women on campus after an incident of molestation.

these movements, which are led particularly by students, are based on ideologies, or are they just a reaction to something?

Sadhguru: See, every human being would like some sense of justice and balance in the situations in which they exist. Whether it's at home, the university, or in the street, you want some sense of equity in what's happening. Even within the home, if there is injustice, many times we fight, isn't it? So the same thing in the university, the same thing on the street, same everywhere.

Let's take family – there is a structure, something is being managed. Your parents are not experts in all kinds of justice systems, ideologies and everything. Out of their love and concern they are just doing what they know best. Is it always perfect? No. Parents are never perfect, isn't it? Maybe you as a young person think what they are doing is no good. But they are doing their best. If they are not doing their best, we can remind them, "You are not doing your best, then I will not do my best if this happens…" Or a more creative way of doing things is when they don't do their best, you really do your best, so that they will feel, "Oh, what am I doing?" Yes, these are different ways to correct a situation.

But there are certain people who think that if a thorn gets into their foot they must cut off the leg. If a thorn got into your foot, what should you do? Carefully remove the thorn and walk on, isn't it? But right now, there are many people who will claim, "Come on, let's amputate the leg!" A campaign will start. Before we protest and deride somebody else or try to pull somebody else down, we must take a little time and see, "Suppose if I am in that place, if all these people are saying a thousand different things, how would I manage?" You must see this. Right now, are the people who are managing the situation some super human beings that they know how to do everything? They don't know. They are trying to do their best. If they are not doing their best, we can key them up a little bit. We should. We should remind them that they should do their best. But expecting a miraculous situation...

In India, if there are three people, there are five opinions, all right? So, we are such a country, where for everything we have a question. When Shiva comes, we throw questions; Krishna comes, we throw questions; whoever comes, we throw thousands of questions – we are that kind of people. It's okay, we're that kind of people. But questioning something is one thing. Always trying to dismantle the existing structure is another thing. If you dismantle the existing structure, are you capable of creating a better structure? This is something you must consider. [*Applause*] Right now, the existing structure may be utterly lousy, but the question is, right now, are we competent, do we have the resources, do we have the time to create a better structure?

The problem right now is we are busy judging everybody. The kind of judgments that we ourselves will not pass. Can I tell you a joke? A lady went into the butcher's shop. You know all those dressed chickens were hanging there. Feathers are the dress of the chicken. They were colorfully dressed, but we pulled off all their feathers, then, for some reason, we say they are dressed! So, these dressed chickens were hanging there – dead, of course. The lady went there, lifted one wing and sniffed, and wrinkled her nose. Then she lifted one leg, wrinkled her nose. Like this she went from chicken to chicken. There were many other customers who were all looking at her and feeling uneasy because of the way she was wrinkling her nose – maybe the chickens are old, getting rotten. The butcher saw that it's going to seriously affect his business, so he went up to her and tapped her on the shoulder. She looked back. He asked, "Ma'am, would you pass a test like that?" [*Laughter*] This is all you have to check – would you pass a test like that?

Saransh: So Sadhguru-ji, when I started saying you are a cool dude... I've been following you since the last three to four years, and you have been doing *Rally for Rivers*, and now you have invented the idea of *Youth and Truth*. And I have seen your video where you are saying that you work for sixteen to twenty hours a day, because you need to work for this country. A lot of responsibility is on you, sir.

Sadhguru: Lot? No, all of it on me. [*Laughter*]

Saransh: So, either you can just transfer some of them to me...

Sadhguru: When you apply, we will consider.

Saransh: *Haan*, I will be applying by tomorrow, sir. So, what I feel is that while sometimes there are people who take on responsibilities, many times people are scared of taking on responsibilities. You have taken the responsibility for rivers, for others, for planting trees, and other things.

Sadhguru: For you also.

Saransh: For me also, *Youth and Truth*. [*Laughs*] But there are times when people are scared of responsibilities.

Sadhguru: See, responsibility – does everybody hear that word clearly? *Responsibility* means *response-ability* – your ability to respond. I am asking you – would you like to retain your ability to respond to every dimension of life that you face?

Audience: Yes.

Sadhguru: Some of you are saying "No." Why? If you don't have the ability to respond, that is when you feel fearful, helpless. If you retain the ability to respond, whatever can be done, you will do. In your life, if you do not do what you cannot do, no problem. But if you do not do what you can do, you're a disaster. I am not a disaster. Everything that I can do, I will do. Will everything happen? Maybe not. Let me tell you how big a failure I am. Is that okay? [*Laughs*]

Actually yesterday, 23rd of September, is thirty-six years since certain things happened within me, and my life changed dramatically. I was going about my business, successful, making money, everything good. But suddenly this experience hit me in such a big way, everything changed. It was on that little hill called Chamundi in Mysore. It was on 23rd of September, 1982. Today, I happen to be in Kashi – thanks to all of you for having me here. [*Applause*] So, when this happened, I was just sitting there simply, doing nothing. Every cell in my body is exploding with ecstasy. I thought, "This is it." I have discovered something that if you don't do anything, you will be overflowing with ecstasy. There's really no problem. At that time, the human population was 5.6 billion people. So I made a plan: in two and a half years' time I will make the entire population blissful, because I know the technology. You don't have to do anything. Simply, if you sit here not doing anything, everything will explode.

See [*pointing at his white beard*], thirty-six years, hm? [*Laughter*] I am still talking to you, not yet gotten you, okay?

Maybe we have touched over five hundred million people, but that's not my idea of the world. There are 7.6 billion people. So, I know I will die a terrible failure, but I will die blissfully, because everything that I can do, I have done.

Saransh: "Successful failure" can be a good word for you.

Sadhguru: No, *blissful* failure. [*Applause*]

Now you have a desire, "My only ambition is I want to build one little house for myself." That happened and you are a success, but a stupid success. My wish for all of you young people is that you must have that kind of a desire which cannot be fulfilled in this life. If your desire for well-being includes everybody, if it is all-inclusive, most probably it will not happen before you die, isn't it? But you took a few steps in that direction, that's great. What is the point of having a constipated desire that is fulfilled in the next five years and you think you are on top of the world? So, I want you to understand that I am wishing you failure but a blissful failure. [*Applause*] The only reason you suffer responsibility is you are always afraid whether it will happen or not happen. Why are you afraid of that? Only because your joy, your happiness, your peacefulness are dependent upon how the world responds to you, not how you are.

First let me ask you this fundamental question. You are referred to as a *human being*. We did not call other creatures "tiger being", "ant being", "elephant being". But, we called this one as "human being". It means this one knows how to *be*. *They* all exist in reaction to outside situations, but this one knows how to be. This is why we know how to respond, not react. This is why this is a responsible creature. If you know how to be, would you keep yourself blissful or miserable? Blissful. If you are blissful, would it really matter what is the consequence of your action? You will do your best. If it happens, it happens; if it doesn't happen, it doesn't happen.

Audience: Yes.

Sadhguru: But when you're shit scared of "what will happen, what will happen, what will happen," you will reduce your desire and responsibility so small. If you are really blissful by your own nature, you know how to be. If you know how to be, does it matter how far your actions go or do not go? Our actions will depend on the times in which we exist, isn't it?

You know, I was at the World Economic Forum. One professor from Harvard University came up to me and said, "Oh, you are that amazing tree planter?" [*Laughter*]

I said, "No, no, I am not a tree planter."

Then he said, "No, no, you planted millions of trees."

"Yes, I did, but I am not a tree planter." [*Laughter*]

Then he asked, "What do you do?"

I said, "I make people flower." [*Applause*]

You know, one day it happened. Two men, government employees, were working. One man was digging pits on the road side, and behind him, another man was closing these pits. Somebody else was passing by and saw this ridiculous activity. They backed up, came up to them and said, "Hey, what are you doing here? This guy is digging pits and this guy is closing them. What is this?"

Then one man said, "No, no, I am doing my job and he is doing his job. The in-between person was the tree planter – he is missing." [*Laughter*]

So because that tree planter has been on a leave for a long time, I stepped in. I am neither a tree planter nor am I a river-saver, okay? Because that person is missing, I stepped in. [*Applause*]

Aditi: Sadhguru, as we grow up, we are often told, or it is fed into our minds since childhood, that life is a race. You need to keep running and be perfect.

Sadhguru: Oh. [*Laughter*] Now, if life is a race, you must win it, isn't it? Winning it means what? You must get to the finish line today. You can choose Manikarnika or Harishchandra Ghat, which one is your choice? [*Applause*] If it's a race, you must cross the finish line ahead of everybody else, isn't it? So whoever is this idiot telling you life is a race, ask them to cross the finish line. [*Laughter*]

Saransh: But what can we say, we are taught like this only. I don't say that the people who taught me were idiots, because… I am on camera. [*Laughter*]

So, I have seen certain godmen also in this country. Sometimes I see that there are many people who are just thronging around the godman and offering *pooja* to him. Once I felt like, why are those people doing pooja to him? But other times, I thought, how powerful and how intelligent that godman is to be able to convince them that "I am a god." So, is this a country where people are so foolish that they are not saying a word and just following a person and treating him like a god, or is that godman so intelligent that he is able to convince them?

Sadhguru: See, just now you said you are on camera and you don't want to call people who say "life is a race" as idiots. But you are calling the whole tradition foolish. [*Laughs*]

Saransh: No, sir, the question…

Sadhguru: No, I will answer the question. See, this word "godman" is a media invented word. I have not seen anybody anywhere who claimed, "I am a godman." I have seen men and I have seen goddamn men. [*Laughter*] I have not seen a godman anywhere. Have you seen a godman anywhere? Anybody? No.

Right now, we garland Malaviya-ji*. Well, is he a god? No, he did something that we revere, that we value, so we offer our respects to him by putting a mala. "Oh, you put a garland on him, so you made a deity out of him." Yes, because the man did something in his life which we all benefited from and value, so we bow down to him. [*Applause*]

See, there is logic of various levels; don't think there is only one logic. There is rudimentary in logic, there is a little higher above, there is also very fine logic. Now, people worship looking up saying, "Our god is up there," and that looks okay to you. This whole *uparwala* business…

The planet is round and spinning all the time. If you look up, inevitably you are looking up in the wrong direction. [*Laughter*] You are not even on the North Pole, you are in Kashi, looking up in the wrong direction all the time, all 360 degrees. Do you know which side is up in this cosmos? Is it marked somewhere, "This side up"? No. So, you don't even know which side is up, but you know *who* is up. I think that's very stupid. Today, in this atom or the cosmos, over 99.999 – whatever number of nines –

---

* Pandit Madan Mohan Malaviya, founder of Banaras Hindu University.

percent is actually empty. There is only a little bit of material in the atom, you know this? I'm sorry, what is your subject?

Saransh: Law.

Sadhguru: Oh, you could argue for all the wrong things.

Saransh: That is what I was waiting for. [*Laughter*]

Sadhguru: Anyway, this is science that over ninety-nine percent of the atom is empty space. Only a little bit is material, a tiny minuscule. The same is true with the cosmos, which has similar proportions – over ninety-nine percent is empty space. Only small specks of stars and planets and galaxies, rest is all empty space. But this empty space seems to have some intelligence of its own, that it keeps all this physical material going around in a certain way. How much ever we study, we see that the physical material itself doesn't carry the needed intelligence; something else is driving it, obviously.

So, the simplistic childish way of coming to it is – there is one man sitting up there and managing everything. But when you look at the size of the cosmos, one man managing things doesn't work, naturally.

Today, women are arguing, "Why can't it be a woman?" I was speaking to a group of people in Nashville in the United States. I was just telling them a joke, and in the joke I referred to God as "He". Immediately ladies stood up. [*Laughter*] They said, "Do you believe God is a man?" Whoa, whoa, whoa, I knew what I'd gotten into. [*Applause*]

I said, "See, I was only telling you a joke."

They said, "It doesn't matter. You said 'him'."

Now in the United States there is a big argument – why can't God be a woman? They tried to settle it in the previous election*. [*Laughter*] But you know the results. Then, there are also arguments like this… Have you heard of Idi Amin, the Uganda man? Idi Amin declared, "God is black." I agree with him. Because if a white man can have a white God, why can't a black man have a black God? [*Applause*] So in the southern churches in the United States, there are actually debates happening whether God is white or black.

We in India know God is brown. [*Laughter*] Yeah, because to those places, God sent only his messenger, son or somebody else. Here, God himself arrived nine times. [*Applause*] Now, especially Indians who are living outside the country are super proud about this. So I keep reminding them that that is because God wouldn't trust anybody else with Indians. [*Laughter*] He knew neither his son, his messenger, nor anybody else would be good for the Indians, so he came hands-on, himself. Nine times, and he failed. See, you can debate whether it has been nine or ten times, but failure is not debatable, isn't it? Failure is very visible.

We can go on endlessly with these things. But your belief systems are culturally relevant, not existentially relevant. You must understand, here we revered people who contributed to our life. Our parents, we bow down to them. If Shiva comes also, this is what you do. If you see a tree, this is what we do; if you see a cow also, this is what we do – even a snake. A cow gave us milk, so we bow down; because the snake didn't bite us today, we bow down. [*Laughter*] I am saying, we are doing the same act

---

* In reference to the US presidential race between Hillary Clinton and Donald Trump.

that we do to God to man, woman, child, animal, everybody. Isn't it so? Then why are you calling a particular man "godman"? We are bowing down to everybody, aren't we? [*Applause*]

Priyanshu: Sadhguru, nowadays youth are so active on social media, and we have been using that platform for various purposes. We even used that for this *Youth and Truth* program, popularizing it here in Varanasi. We asked for several questions on the social media also and selected the most popular ones out of those questions. So I have one question.

It is Pranav who asks, "At home they teach us how to behave with girls, but when I go out with my friends, we see something which is totally different. When I go online, things are crazy. How is a man supposed to behave with or treat a woman?"

Sadhguru: Well, a woman is not a separate species, first of all. [*Applause*] Too much of this man-woman thing is being done, unfortunately. It's a small biological difference to serve a certain purpose. We are all here today because of this difference, yes? Because we have a mother and a father – one happens to be a woman in that – because of that, we are born and we are here. So, we don't have to treat women like a separate species.

We must understand this – there was a time when a woman couldn't really go out and do much because of the nature of the world around her. You know, around 3000 people turned up from many parts of the world for yesterday's event in Kashi*. I think more than sixty percent were women. Now, suppose this was 1000 years ago, it would be ninety-five percent men and maybe only five percent women. Because to travel on foot or

---

* A satsang on Sadhguru's Enlightenment Day.

on a horseback and come to Kashi from a thousand miles away would be a challenging thing and not very safe for a woman. But today, you must understand, it's not your liberal attitude which has brought woman reasonably level with men – it's just technology.

Technology has levelled the difference because your big muscle is no more useful – you need some brain. [*Applause*] There was a time when man's muscle did everything on this planet, and naturally man was dominant. This dominance also is misunderstood. He dominated in one arena which was filmed and reported; she dominated in a different arena which was private and not reported. [*Applause*]

This controversy has been going on with me for the last ten days, because I said if you make economics or money the prime value of your life, then the world will become very masculine as there will be no room for the feminine to find expression. They may be women, but they will surrender their feminine to be successful, unfortunately. This should not happen. Women should succeed as women, not as men – with full-blown feminine nature they must be able to be successful in a society. They don't have to pretend to be a man to be successful. If this has to go, the world has to move completely from brawn to brain; this transition is very important. [*Applause*]

Now when you talk about economy or money power, it's brawn. Money is another kind of muscle. We are taking away the physical muscle and bringing in the money muscle. So, once again you are creating a masculine dominated society, because now women have understood how to be successful by being masculine. This is not a good thing for the world. There must be a world where women can be hundred percent feminine and still be absolutely successful. If this has to happen, money should not be the ruling factor; it should be just currency. But right now, money is the ruling factor, so the masculine becomes the dominant force. We need to change this. Unless music, aesthetics, love, beauty and other things become equal in proportion, the feminine will not flourish. And if the feminine is wiped out of this planet, then all the men will sit and wonder, "Why are we living?" [*Applause*]

Aditi: Sadhguru, in your AV* you said it was difficult for you to plant trees in people's minds, and then rest of the things just happened. So I want to ask, how do we plant this seed in their minds that females need to flourish as females?

Sadhguru: See, you don't have to plant it in their heads, you have to plant it in your head. [*Applause*]

Aditi: But like I said in my first question, yes, we can do it on our part, but then there is society – there are ways that people judge us.

Sadhguru: See, don't think there is no judgment for a male. Don't think there is no exploitation for a male. It is there. It is just that for a woman, unfortunately, any little exploitation takes on a sexual tone, all right? That is the ugly part of it. Otherwise, men are exploited in many different ways – ask him [*points to Saransh*]. [*Laughter*] That is why a lawyer is successful, because somebody is exploited, isn't it?

---

* Introductory video about Sadhguru shown to the audience just before the main talk.

Saransh: I want to say thank you, sir, for saying this.

Sadhguru: The problem is we are still in such a consciousness that we will exploit anything that's weaker than us – man, woman, child or animal. Yes or no? Because still we don't have brain in our head; we have muscle in our head, okay? The muscle should transform into brain cells; then we will see that for you to succeed you don't have to really exploit anything, actually. In fact, if you get the love and cooperation of everybody, you will succeed even better.

I will tell you an example. I was doing a program for one of the top international companies. Twenty-five of their top executives were there. It's a three-day event and I had nine volunteers. I don't know if you noticed our volunteers here. Without one instruction, they just go about doing everything that needs to be done. If something is not done, I know it could not be done. There is no question of somebody not having done it, because we've built such a force. [*Applause*] So, they watched these nine people moving around. Then they asked, "Sadhguru, where do you get such people?" Because they are always looking for attrition, you know?

Then I said, "You don't get them, you got to make them."

"How do you make them?"

I said, "You have to make them fall in love with you."

"Oh, how do you do that?"

I said, "First you must fall in love with them." [*Applause*]

Then they say, "Oh, they don't pay us for that." [*Laughter*]

So, when money is the only ruling factor in your life, you are like a circus monkey. If I give a banana you will jump; otherwise you will simply sit. So, if you are not a circus monkey, then you will see exploiting is not a good thing. If everybody falls in love with you, how easy and wonderful it is to work. When people hate you, when they resent you, they will make your life miserable, believe me. When you are resentful about somebody and you have to work for them, won't you make sure their life is miserable? Yes. This is why people are thinking work is so stressful – because everybody hates them. If they create a really loving and inclusive atmosphere around them where there is no sense of exploitation…

See, I don't exploit anybody, but I work them to death. [*Laughter*] But before that, I am working myself. People are afraid I may kill myself so they're also trying to catch up. There is no problem. If I sit like this [*lounges back on the chair*] and make you work, then you will come up with something else to make my life miserable. When you see you're only emulating me, then why will you feel exploited? I make them work seven days of the week, eighteen hours a day non-stop. Day or night. At two o'clock in the morning I will call them and say, "Do this, do that, do that," because so many things are happening. [*Pointing to Saransh*] See, you are joining up, so I am telling you. [*Laughter*]

Saransh: Yes, yes.

Sadhguru: So, exploitation is a silly, unintelligent way of doing things in the world. Inclusiveness is the best way to do work in the world. You know, we are a volunteer organization, over 4600 full-time volunteers and over nine million part-time volunteers. Every day somebody comes up to me and says, "Sadhguru, I can't work with this person, she is terrible, he is like this, he is like that."

I say, "See, in this world there are only these kinds of people. If you think what you are doing is very significant, you have to work with these kinds of people. But if you think you want to work with *ideal* people, you must go to heaven – and today." [*Laughter*]

If you think what you are doing is very significant, you will work with whatever you have. If you have donkeys, you will work with them, yes? But you have not realized the significance of what you are doing, and now you are busy complaining about everything. This doesn't mean everything around me is perfect, but everybody is doing their best, that's all. [*Applause*]

Saransh: Sadhguru, in social media, certain news spreads; it's just forwarded to certain groups and then certain other things occur. People think that these messages are real, and they just try to do what the message says. So Madhusudan-ji, has asked, "Is there a line of separation between thinking and overthinking?"

Sadhguru: [*Laughs*] See, I don't know if you have seen the byline for *Youth and Truth*. We're talking about exploring truth not with the seriousness of a gospel but with the playfulness of gossip. Gossip has been the most reliable system of seeking truth, yes or no? If the official thing comes out, you will ask around with your friends and neighbors, "What happened? Is this true?" Everybody says five different things. Then you find your own filter for that and arrive at, "Okay, this is what should have happened." So social media is new; it means gossip has gone global suddenly. Gossip was always there locally. Yes or no?

Audience: Yes.

Sadhguru: Ladies, tell me. [*Laughter*] Because more people confide in you. A man is walking like this [*gestures marching*], so nobody wants to talk to him. A woman is paying attention and walking, so they will talk to her. [*Laughs*] Gossip has always been there in every society, and it's a reliable thing. But now, suddenly, gossip has gone global because of technology. This globalization of gossip has caused a little bit of disruption and the scale of things that happen is a little disproportionate to what we were used to. Earlier, by the time we told ten people, it would have died down. Today, one forward, *boom!* Two hundred and fifty people got it in the town. It could incite certain things.

Well, many people have used it well. Some people have misused it. This is true with anything. Right now, we can use this vessel [*referring to the copper pot next to him*] to store water, or I can take it and smash it on your head. So, now shall we ban all the copper vessels because somebody's skull got cracked? No, so we have to culture the society. Educating and evolving the society is not going to happen overnight. If something is going out of control, maybe a little enforcement is needed. But just clamping down on anything and everything that causes a little damage is not the way.

For example, I am from Mysore. When I was just thirteen-and-a-half years of age, I got enough money, put gas into my father's scooter and went to Bangalore without him knowing, made a circle there and came back all the way. It was a single-track road with potholes, and many times I had to ride standing because of various things – one being height. [*Laughs*] Later on, when we graduated to motorcycles, if we thought about it, we could just go *boom boom,* and in one hour and thirty-five minutes, we would do 140 kilometers and come back.

But now, they put a six-lane highway, and traffic started moving fast. They did not bypass the villages because of land acquisition. They went on expanding the existing road. There are lots of villages, and people get killed crossing the road, unfortunately. A lot of pedestrians get killed in India because they don't know where to cross, or they can't judge the speed, or they are just so full of themselves. They come in the way and they expect somebody to stop. So, they went on putting road bumps. In 140 kilometers of road, they put over 120 road bumps.

So, you got a six-lane highway, but you cannot even get to third gear. What is the point? We could have a mud track. Why are you spending money on the highway? Now, by High Court order, it's all being removed, but the villages will put up their own road bumps. They will not learn how to cross the road. This culture must go.

Some damage happens because of somebody's irresponsible action. Instead of fixing that irresponsibility, we want to destroy the possibility. Many wonderful things have been done on social media, but now somebody gets killed because of somebody's mischief, so we want to ban that. This is not the way to do things. This is not the way to take the nation forward. Unfortunately, it is true, some people pay the price, but we must bring more responsible usage of that, rather than simply banning this and that. [*Applause*]

Aditi: One more question that came through the social media was: You told Ranveer [Singh] that ambition is limited. It is a thought and not worth investing our life in. Without goals or commitment or destination, how will I even take my next step? And you also had the goal of Dhyanalinga. I am really confused.

Sadhguru: [*Laughs*] I think one part of that we've already answered. See, what you call ambition is essentially a thought that you generated, isn't it? How did you generate this thought? Maybe people around you influenced you, or above all, essentially your ambition or your thought is only coming from the limited data that you already possess. Many of you are in your early twenties – do you believe you have already collected data about everything that you need to know about the world, all the possibilities that life may hold? No. With what little you know, if you fix your life's goal, I think that'll be a poor life. Right now, you are in college, you can fix a goal: "Within the stipulated period I want to get out of the college. [*Laughter*] Not too early because they threw me out, not too late because I didn't get out." Yes? How I want to get out – whether I want to get out with first class or this or that, how much I should know – that is a goal you can set because already it's a structured time. In this structured time, you set a goal. But you don't set a goal for your life ruling out all the possibilities that may open up.

So, ambition means you got committed to a single idea which came from very limited data in your life, isn't it? Don't get committed to a limited idea. Limited ideas are okay in the short term. "Right now, I am here for five years in this university. This is what I want to do in these five years." This is okay. But life must unfold. You must give it an opportunity to unfold.

Only reason why you are committing yourself like this is you are afraid of uncertainty. You think certainty has come because you pegged it there – "I am going to be a doctor" at the age of three. This certainty is death-like certainty because it takes away all possibilities. The many possibilities of life should be explored; only then human genius will unfold and we will have multifaceted human beings in the country.

Aditi: Like you said, we should set specific goals for a short time. If we are setting a goal, we will definitely work very hard for it, but in due course, we see people amongst us or we ourselves might resort to some unhealthy practices just because this is set in our minds that "Okay, this is my goal. I want to achieve it."

Sadhguru: What is an unhealthy practice?

Aditi: Like a foul competitive streak amongst our fellow classmates. It could be like pulling someone else down just to go ahead.

Sadhguru: No, if you pull somebody else down, you do not go ahead; both of you go back. [*Applause*] This is what I said. If something has to unfold within you, the outside should not decide everything. The outside will decide a few things; the rest should come from within. That's what a human being means. For other creatures, everything is decided by reaction to the outside; for a human being there is enough intelligence that a whole lot of things have to come from within, not from reactions to the outside. So, if you keep looking at how somebody else is doing, now obviously you will take a misstep.

Somebody was asking me, "Sadhguru, how can we beat the Pakistani team?"

I said, "Don't beat the Pakistani team, just hit the damn ball." [*Applause*] You don't try to go and beat Pakistan with a cricket bat. With a cricket bat you just hit the damn ball. There is no Pakistan in the ball. You just have to hit the ball so that the Pakistanis will not find the ball. But if you are looking at a Pakistani and wanting to beat him, the ball may smash your face. [*Laughs*]

Why are you bothered how somebody else is doing? Are you doing your best or not? That's all the question is with life. [*Looking at Saransh*] Even if you want to become a mystic, you know, don't worry about me.

Saransh: Why shouldn't I worry, sir? You are the competitor if I want to become the mystic.

Sadhguru: [*Laughs*] No, I am not in competition with you, but I must tell you this, because there is an aspiration – it's nice. It once happened, Shankaran Pillai went to the bar. Once a couple of drops go inside, the stories get taller and taller, you know. Everybody was saying big things about their families and stuff. So Shankaran Pillai waited, and then they nudged him, "Hey! What, you got nothing to say? No good!"

He said, "No, my uncle was a great mystic. He knew the exact time, date and mode of death in his life."

"Oh, really? He knew the time, date and how he will die well ahead of time?"

He said, "Yes, my uncle, a great mystic!"

"Really? How did he come to know?"

"The judge told him." [*Laughter*]

[*Speaking to Saransh*] See, there is a possibility, hm? [*Laughs*]

Saransh: You have drifted the whole thing into law, that's a nice way. [*Laughter*] So Sadhguru-ji, I would also like to open the floor to certain questions from the audience. Since we have a time constraint, we will be taking only two questions.

Ayushi: Namaskaram, Sadhguru! I'm Ayushi Dixit, third-year Political Science student. Sadhguru, today, on the one hand, we see all these scientific, psychological methods, whereas on the other side, we have spirituality and mysticism. So how can we make these factors collaborate and have a better governance and a better society?

Sadhguru: Do you think governance needs psychological treatment? [*Laughter*]

Ayushi: Yes, there are concepts in political science that work psychologically also.

Sadhguru: Okay. [*Laughs*] See, this is a culture where the spiritual leaders always largely worked with the kings of the time. Not because they wanted to bum around in the palaces and get some benefits, but simply because they saw unless you benefit the man who has the power to make a difference to millions of people, people will not really benefit. If you get to a position of responsibility or power where every word you utter, every thought, every emotion, and every action that you perform has influence over millions of people, then the first and foremost thing you need to do is to fix yourself, so that how you think, feel, speak and act is calibrated for the well-being of the people.

This is why Krishna's whole life was just about marrying the political system and the spiritual process. You take Gautama Buddha, he was working with kings. Otherwise, you can work from the bottom up, but that's a *long* way. Today, it is possible because we have communication.

I want you to imagine. When a Gautama walked from village to village, if he spoke, not even ten people would hear him. Forty years of his enlightened life he walked and walked village to village, but impact was not good. He knew that, so he went to the kings and tried to impact them, because once they are impacted, they will change things in the nation. Monarchy is a kind of autocratic rule, so if the king gets it, he will make sure something happens. In a democratic process, it is not as impactful; here, people are the leaders. Fortunately, today we have the ability to communicate like never before. We can sit here and talk to the whole world if we want. This was never possible before.

Many great beings have come, but unfortunately when they spoke, hardly fifty people could hear. And even if they heard, somebody wrote it down all wrong. After 1000 years, another hundred people modified it in so many different ways; by the time it comes to you after 2000 years, you don't know what the hell is coming to you. But today, see, these cameras are recording. If you say something different from what I said, they will play the video. This was never possible before. Now we can work from the grassroots. But at that time, the only way to work was top-down, because only the top was possible to reach, not down. Today we can work both ways, but ground up is more effective. That is why we are working with people.

So, between psychology and spirituality, what is the difference? See, with psychology you are essentially trying to analyze the mechanics of the thought and emotion in a certain way. But in the spiritual cultures of India, we don't give any significance to your thought. You can think what you want; we know it's just the surface of who you are. Because thought is coming only from the limited data that you have gathered, isn't it so?

But your behavioral patterns are coming from dimensions much deeper than thought. If you've ever been a little psychologically disturbed, suddenly you can see that something else beyond what you have known, beyond your regular thought and emotional patterns, is influencing you and pushing you and pulling you in ways that you can't help yourself. Yes or no? If it's not happened to you, you may have seen such people.

We don't pay any attention to your present thoughts and emotions, because we see these are acquired patterns which have happened because of the data you have gathered. But there are other dimensions of influence within you which we wish to bring balance to. For this, you need willingness and you have to work with people.

With psychology also, you have to endlessly talk, but most people cannot be talked out of anything; they will talk *you* out of it. [*Laughs*] So when counseling doesn't work, you have chemical bombing – you put chemicals into the system in the form of pills or whatever, which could bring balance. Because, after all, human experience is rooted in chemistry; it has a chemical basis to it. Modern psychiatry is looking at how to manage human chemistry by putting in outside ingredients. Well, when things have gone to the extreme, that's the way to do it. If things are reasonably in control, we have systems by which one can work oneself out of it. So, we are looking at how to manage one's chemistry without taking external inputs.

Sushanth: A very good afternoon, sir. My name is Sushanth Kumar Bishwa. I am a research scholar from BHU and am very much fortunate to have time to clear my doubt from you, sir. You know, seven years back, when I got admission in BHU, in a very small diploma course, just part time…

Sadhguru: What course?

Sushanth: Diploma in tourism management. I was very happy to get enrolled in that course. I went to my father shouting like anything that I got admission in BHU; it was as though I had cracked IIM Ahmedabad. Now, after seven years, I have cracked NET and got admitted to a PhD program But I am not happy with what I am doing, sir. Because I have lost my spark. I have lost my motivation. How to regain that, to live my life in a joyful way, to regain my inner peace? Thank you, sir.

Sadhguru: See, the nature of life is such, if you go outside in the garden and try to catch an ant – the BHU ant, who is born here, who's grown up here and probably will die here – will he say, "Okay, to hell with my life, crush me if you want"? He'll do everything to protect himself. He values his life very much, isn't it? He's a tiny little creature that we may not even notice. We may step on him without even seeing him, but he values his life immensely. Yes or no?

Audience: Yes.

Sadhguru: He's got spark. But you, a human being, are the peak of evolution on this planet, at least physiologically, yes? About behavioral aspects, we may have questions, but physiologically you are *the* most evolved creature on the planet. You have a very vivid sense of memory and a fantastic sense of imagination. An ant doesn't have such a vivid sense of memory, nor does he have any great imagination. He has some, but he has a presence of mind about the life that he is living.

The education system that you are going through right from kindergarten level is such that it is about everything else except *you*. Somebody is PhD in tourism, PhD in biotechnology,

PhD in something else, but nothing about this one [*referring to oneself*]. There is no attention at all as to how does this one function.

You know, you have a Kala Bhairava Temple here. What this means is, a human being exists in three times. He lives because of the richness of his memory – how rich your memory is determines what you will do and what you will not do right now, isn't it so? So memory is important. The present experience is important. And how vivid your imagination is for tomorrow is very important. The problem is, these things have all gotten mixed up simply because there is no discipline of faculty, so your own mind turns against you. What happened ten years ago you still suffer and what may happen day after tomorrow you already suffer, because there is no discipline of faculty.

You don't know how to use your memory, you don't know how to use your imagination. Your memory makes you suffer, your imagination makes you suffer, and you think you are suffering your life. You are not suffering your life; you are only suffering the two greatest faculties of being human – a vivid sense of memory and a fantastic sense of imagination. If you suffer the greatest faculties that you have, what can we do with you? If you suffer an ailment – understandable; if you suffer a disability – understandable; if you suffer your ability – hopeless case. [*Laughter*] Yes or no?

Audience: Yes.

Sadhguru: You are suffering your capabilities. I must tell you this. About five months ago, I think… you might have seen it on the news. A thirty-four-year-old lady, who was a television anchor in Hyderabad, jumped out of the fifth-floor window and killed herself. She left a note – "Nobody is responsible for my death, my brain is my enemy." How many million years it took to get this brain to this size and now it becomes your enemy! She articulated this, but this is true with almost ninety percent of human beings. They are suffering their own intelligence, isn't it? If you take away half their brain, they will be peaceful. And that is why a whole bunch of idiots are going about saying that the ultimate goal of life is peace of mind. Such people will only rest in peace. [*Applause*]

Now you, young man, they have kept you here for too long – seven years! They should have thrown you out in four years, then you would have done something. [*Laughs*] During university life, if somebody is not keying you up all the time, it could become too easy, you know. Even I remember, when I went to the university, most of the time we were in the canteen or in the garden. The easiest part of my life was university. [*Applause*] I know nobody is going to like it, but I think this university time must be shortened. If somebody is doing something very focused and very intense, producing something brilliant, they must stay. Otherwise, everybody must be chucked out within three to four years' time. [*Applause*]

This is all I am telling you young people: do whatever the hell you want in your life, but you must be intensely focused on something. If you are not investing your life in anything, it will just go waste, because one basic ingredient of your life is time. This is just going away. Already you are two hours closer to your grave since I came here. Two hours closer to Manikarnika. [*Laughter*] Yes or no?

Audience: Yes.

Sadhguru: Yes, you are not immortal. It's just a limited amount of time. I am asking, is your life precious to you?

Audience: Yes.

Sadhguru: If this is worthless, throw it somewhere. If this is precious, then you must decide where you want to invest this life. If you invest this in something worthwhile – not spark, you will be aflame all the time. [*Laughs*]

Saransh: That's what my first question was about. I am investing it in a good one, being a mystic.

Sadhguru: Because you are a lawyer, the judge may tell you. [*Laughter*]

Aditi: As you said that time is limited, so we are approaching the end of this wonderful gossip. I would like to thank you for spending your time, because if time is money then you have spent millions on us today. [*Applause*]

Sadhguru: Hey, no, no. Let me correct you. Time is not money, time is life! What is this! See, she is already a practicing dentist – money, money, money. [*Applause*]

Priyanshu: Sadhguru, I do not have the words to express my gratitude. The only thing is, if somebody asks me what we have got in Kashi, now I can answer, "Once, I had Sadhguru here." [*Sadhguru laughs*] Thank you very much for coming to us. [*Saransh is about to say something*]

Sadhguru: Hey, the end is the judge [*pointing to himself*], not the lawyer [*pointing to Saransh*]. [*Laughter*]

Saransh: [*Pointing to the audience*] I think one phone rang, and you had said that when you hear that song*, you dance. And I saw your video with Ranveer Singh**, sir. So, can we have that? [*Cheers*] Because this is the Shiv Nagari, and we just sing it every time. Sir, please if we can? That's your favorite one.

Sadhguru: [*Laughs*] Music will come, we'll wait. I want to see the young people dance and then we will see.

I want all of you to understand we are living in a country where still millions of people, nearly five hundred million people probably don't even get to eat properly, all right? In such a country, all of us have the privilege that at least we don't have to search for our food. And not just that, you are in a premier institution like BHU – thanks to Malaviya-ji for creating this. [*Applause*]

When the British left, we were nearly ninety percent illiterate. At that time, somebody had the vision to educate India, and you are part of this great institution. I want you to always appreciate the privilege that you are here, a privilege which *so* many others in this country have not found. Please make use of this time at the university to build yourself. Don't worry about the nation, the society, this and that. Build yourself into a grand human being, because if there are no great human beings, there'll be no great society. If there is no society, there's no great nation. If there are no great nations, there is no great world. So, you can't build a great world or a great nation. You can only make

---

* "*Alai Alai*" by Sounds of Isha.
** *In Conversation with the Mystic* event with Ranveer Singh, in which Sadhguru danced.

yourself into a great human being and, around you, wonderful things will happen. It's my wish and my blessing the best should happen to you. Thank you very much. [*Applause*]

Saransh: What about the dance, sir?

Sadhguru: Hey, lawyer's job is over. Now, it's the judge. [*Laughter*]

IN THE CITY OF LIGHT

In 2017, Saransh, a law student at Banaras Hindu University, had written several emails to Sadhguru's Office inviting Sadhguru to speak at his college campus, but Sadhguru could not make it due to his busy schedule. In July 2018, when Saransh received a phone call from Isha Foundation, he got what he was desperately waiting for. "I informed Saransh and the head of the Law Department at BHU that Sadhguru will visit Kashi on his 36th Enlightenment Day (23 September 2018), and that there will be an opportunity to host him for a live conversation with students at their campus," shares Vidhya Vinodhini, an Isha Yoga instructor.

Soon, Saransh took up the task of organizing the event, starting with spreading the word: "Without revealing the date of Sadhguru's visit, we created a Facebook event page, and made sure we informed every college and hostel on the campus through various means. When we announced the date, curiosity multiplied."

As more students joined hands with the organizing team, Saransh and Isha volunteers curated street plays (or *nukkad natak*, as they are called in northern India) to publicize the event. Skits were performed near the Vishwanath temple, around cafeterias at the BHU campus, at parks, and the Assi Ghat, a popular student hangout. "The skits created huge excitement. Every single student and faculty member we met was eagerly looking forward to it," Saransh says.

SLEEPLESS NIGHTS AND MIDNIGHT CHAI

The students who were part of the organizing team were busy attending classes and studying during the day, so they spent their late nights promoting and planning the event execution. The only support they needed to stay up were pots of hot ginger tea, which their hostel mess readily agreed to provide every night.

"We had several sleepless nights, yet nobody in our team skipped a single class during the day," recounts Saransh. "We put up banners at the campus until 2 or 3 a.m., and held meetings with students over dinner in the hostel mess. Often, we would even knock on hostel doors in the middle of the night to spread awareness, but seeing Sadhguru's photo on the poster, they would say, 'Okay, come in. Let's talk about it.'" He adds, "We personally met and interacted with over ninety percent of the students on BHU campus."

THE PROBLEM OF PLENTY!

Vidhya had the responsibility of coordinating all the northern Indian centers for Isha, including Kashi. To ensure smooth execution of an elaborate event plan, she decided to stay in a BHU hostel for twenty-five days and worked closely with the student organizing team.

One challenge before them was to find a venue that could accommodate a few thousand people at once. The largest auditorium at BHU (with a 3000-seating capacity) was under maintenance, so they had to settle for a smaller 500-capacity venue. But seeing the volume of registrations pouring in, the organizing team knew this wouldn't be enough. They then transformed a parking ground nearby into a temporary outdoor auditorium with a large LED screen to accommodate 1000 eager students.

Despite all measures, the team fell woefully short of students' expectations. Long serpentine queues of students and faculty members started appearing four hours before the event. "After we opened the doors, the auditorium filled up in less than five minutes!" Vidhya exclaims. Yet, over 5000 students were still queued up outside the auditorium, hoping to get in. "To escort Sadhguru inside the venue was an uphill task," she admits, "as he was surrounded by thousands of student-fans who wanted to shake hands or take selfies."

Sadhguru was accorded a rousing welcome on stage with "Har Har Mahadev" slogans. The much-awaited conversation went on for nearly two hours and ended on an unexpected but wonderful note. Aditi, one of the moderators, shares, "It was a highly exuberant atmosphere and the only one in the *Youth and Truth* series where we witnessed Sadhguru dance on the stage with students."

A TRIBUTE TO PANDIT MADAN MOHAN MALAVIYA

To honor Pandit Malaviya, the founder of BHU, and his immense contributions, Sadhguru was keen to do another event at the varsity – and the Pandit's house-turned-museum was a natural choice for the venue. "We thought inviting students from the Music and Dance departments for this event would be most appropriate, as Kashi has been home to a rich tradition and history of music and dance, from poet-saint Kabir to Shehnai player Bismillah Khan, Kathak maestro Birju Maharaj and several luminaries in between," shares Anand, an Isha volunteer and then a third-year Computer Science student.

"Several students sang their hearts out, and asked Sadhguru questions on these intricate artforms which mainstream educational institutions usually don't dwell upon," notes Aditi. Sadhguru explained how the classical arts were designed to take one towards ultimate liberation – the very purpose for which Kashi was built.

AN UNFORGETTABLE EXPERIENCE

"One instance that clearly stands out in my memory is Sadhguru's insistence to ask whatever questions we wished. I found this atypical of a guru and was taken aback. Also, women are expected to be unquestioning and put on a gentle demeanor. These are unsaid rules of the society and family I grew up in. But Sadhguru shattered all myths about gurus, and my own limitations that were holding me back from asking the deepest questions of my life," confesses Aditi.

"After the BHU event, Sadhguru has become a household name in Kashi. Soon, we started receiving requests from many educational institutes and other groups to conduct similar programs on their campuses," says Vidhya.

Saransh sums up the response: "I studied at the BHU campus for five years until 2019, but never witnessed the level of enthusiasm and participation from students for any event before or after *Youth and Truth*. It was truly unprecedented. It's been more than three years since the event, but it feels like it happened yesterday. The memory of it and the preparations that preceded it are etched in my heart and mind."

"Youth is a state of tremendous energy. This could be transformed into a beautiful or ugly expression of humanity, a great possibility or a disaster."

COLUMBIA BUSINESS SCHOOL, NEW YORK

29 April 2019

Varud* **(Moderator)**: Today, we're going to talk about two different buckets. One is about the self, and the other is self's context within society. Between those two, there's a very common theme of figuring out what our purpose is within self and society. I think it's something that a lot of our generation faces – it's dubbed "the millennial existential crisis" – something that I've been through myself. So to start off today, we want to figure out, when it comes to purpose, what has defined your purpose in this world? As it has led to you being here at the Columbia Business School and the *Youth and Truth* program. And, if you have any words for other people in the audience, or

---

* Co-author with Devang Singh of the cookbook *Bhagwaan Ke Pakwaan: Food of the Gods.*

just me would be fine as well, around how do we find purpose in this world?

Sadhguru: Talking about buckets, I think you should kick the bucket because self and society are not entirely two different things. So many people put together is society, isn't it? Just a word. When we do not want to address you as an individual, but we want to address you as a group of people, we say this is a society. But that's just a word.

If you really come down to it, there are just individual people. Well, a certain group of people may agree upon a few aspects and they may think they are one society. But if you go further down, people are just people, individuals are just individuals. You can't really merge them and say these are all one kind. There's no such thing. Maybe there are a few things that they agree upon which makes them into various kinds of societies. If you're a secret society, maybe there are more things that you agree upon.

When we see that to address issues in the world we cannot go about addressing individuals, then we make a society; when we find that a society is still not an effective way to handle them, then we make it a nation; when we see that is also not an effective way, then we make a global situation or an international forum. So, this is only in terms of how to find a larger solution. A larger solution is something individuals will always disagree with on so many different levels, isn't it? Is there any one thing on the planet that all of us agree on? There is no such thing. Individual people always disagree on something. But we also agree that it's all right, because it seems to be working for everybody. I don't like the speed limit in America, but I agree with it because all sorts of people are driving. All right, I'll drive

at seventy miles, and once in a way I get heavy on the right leg…
but fine. [*Laughs*]

So, you're asking, what is the mission? If this same question
was asked in a different situation… in a way this also borders
on when people ask, "What is the God-given purpose of my
life?" Whatever is the source of creation, what makes you think
the source of creation which created this cosmos – you do not
know where it begins or ends – is even keeping account of you?
Forget about giving you a specific purpose, maybe the source of
this creation doesn't even know you exist.

Because this very solar system is a tiny little speck in this
cosmic space, isn't it? Tomorrow morning, believe me, if the
entire solar system evaporates, nobody will notice it. That's how
small it is. In that speck, planet Earth is a micro-speck. New
York City is a super, super micro-speck. In that, you are a big
man. This is a serious problem. [*Laughs*]

You think there is a God-given purpose for you – this is
the peak of human arrogance. All this is coming from the basis
that has been spread in the name of religion and faith, that the
existence is human-centric. Existence is not human-centric;
we're just one more creature which happened recently, according
to the evolutionary sciences. Yes? If you do not know this… if
all the worms disappear today, in twelve to eighteen months,
all life will cease on this planet. If all the insects disappear, in
somewhere between four and a half to six years, all life will cease
on this planet. But if all the human beings disappear, the planet
will flourish.

This sense of self-assumed significance that people have
brought to themselves has made us walk with absolute

insensitivity on this planet. Absolutely insensitive to every other life, because we think everything is here to serve us. Ask an ant, does it want to serve you? Go sit on an anthill and check whether it wants to serve you. It doesn't want to serve you. It doesn't matter what kind of books you write for yourself, the ants don't believe it. If you don't understand this about the ants, then come to the southern Indian forest – the tigers definitely don't believe that they are here to serve you; you will be served to them. [*Laughs*]

So, we must give up this idea, because wherever it was propagated that "I'm fulfilling a God-given purpose," people did the most horrendous things. So, we are here as human societies, and we have issues, problems, struggles. Whatever you think needs to be sorted out and whatever you think is within your aptitude to sort out, it's time you pick that damn thing up and sort it out. It's not any God-given mission. You got to do something, so do something useful because there is some joy in solving something.

This is all the choice we have – you can either be a part of the problem or be part of the solution. If you enjoy being part of the problem, do it – there will be consequences. Sometimes it's fun to create problems. Yes, it is, but it will have its own kind of consequences. The only thing you have to learn is, do whatever the hell you want, just do it well. But for every action you perform, there is a consequence. When the consequence comes your way, if you're able to joyfully go through it, you can do anything you wish. But when the consequence comes, if you're the kind that cries, then you must control your action.

Adrianna (Moderator): What if you're just a crybaby, though?

Sadhguru: If you're a baby, you must be with your mother. [*Laughter*]

Adrianna: So, on the note of purpose, one thing that I think I'm constantly chasing is, and I don't know when I've reached it, is the pursuit of happiness. I think everyone in this room, at some point, may be asking themselves why it can be elusive. For me, happiness stems from my family; they're such a critical piece to my love and happiness. But oftentimes, I feel like I lose sight of it when I'm at Columbia Business School, when I'm at work, because I'm trying to get to that next level – ultimately to help my family. But how do we keep track of what's most important, that purpose for me being my family, and the pursuit of happiness?

Sadhguru: See, you're of Mexican origin. Family may mean a different thing to you. Ask Alex – family means crime! [*Laughter*]

Alexander (Moderator): Ah… with tears of laughter! Oh, you know, my parents are here. [*Laughter*]

Sadhguru: No, no, a few decades ago, when the Italians said "family" it meant crime, all right.

Family is the smallest unit of a society. But if you get overly identified with it, you will become a crime. All the crime that we commit on this planet – only human beings commit crimes, nobody else does. What you call as evil, genocide, prejudice, have all come because of limited identifications that each one of us hold. "This is my family, this is my race, this is my religion, this is my nation" – it is from this that all the terrible things happen on the planet, isn't it? People who are doing this believe, at that moment, they're just doing the right thing. This is what identity does to you.

You need to understand the very structure of human intelligence. There are different dimensions of intelligence. Unfortunately today, in education systems we are exploring only one, which is the intellect. If I ask you a simple question – please, you must answer this because I'm going to bless you at the end of the answer – would you want your intellect to be sharp or blunt?

Audience: Sharp.

Sadhguru: Only if it is sharp it works well, because it's a cutting instrument. Yes? It can only dissect. Now you're using this intellect to do everything. To cut, it's okay; but if you want to stitch with it, you will be in tatters. Is that the reason why all the trousers are going into tatters? [*Laughs*] Essentially, if you try to use a cutting instrument on everything, it can cause a lot of misery.

Right now, please see, for most of you… [*pointing to Alexander*] even though you're from Brooklyn, nobody ever stabbed you with a dagger, isn't it?

Alexander: Not yet. [*Laughs*]

Sadhguru: They ignored you. So, I'm asking, how much physical suffering has actually come from outside? Almost nothing. Rest is all on self-help. You sit by yourself [*gestures stabbing oneself*]… Why? Because we gave you a sharp intellect. If we had given you the brain of an earthworm, you would be fine. The problem is just this: we have a cerebral capability which most human beings have not learnt how to handle. You can call this stress, anxiety, misery, cruelty, murder, you can call it whatever. Essentially, all that's happened is your intelligence has turned against you. Why has this happened? Simply because of limited identities that you have taken. It may look great – my family, my nation. See, if you're strongly identified with something, you're willing to die for it, isn't it?

Audience: Yes.

Sadhguru: If you're willing to die for it, you are also willing to kill for it. Yes or no?

Audience: Yes.

Sadhguru: Whatever you're willing to die for, you're also willing to kill for – isn't that the only problem we have on this planet right now? Everybody's willing to die for something and everybody's willing to kill for something. It could be family, nation, race, religion, whatever. Is it not time that you upgrade how you identify yourself and with what you identify yourself?

In traditional education in India, we believed that – even now we do this to some extent – from zero to twelve years of age, there is not any kind of learning. The child should just play well, eat well, sleep well – because our intent is that the brain should grow to a reasonable size before we load it with something. It's a sensible thing. But no, today they want speed learning at the age of three. Some people are talking about how to teach the child mathematics when the mother is pregnant! [*Laughter*] So, till twelve years of age, we don't want to teach the child anything, except to eat well, to play well, and to sleep. Because these three things will decide how your body and your brain grow.

Before we start the education process, there is something done to fix the identity of the child. They will start chanting a mantra: *Aham brahmasmi*. This means "My identity is cosmic". My identification is not with my family, not with my father and mother, not with my nation, not with my religion, not even global; my identity is with the cosmos.

See, if your identity is not with any limited thing, if you walked into this room, you'd actually have no problem just like that with anybody. You may get into trouble later, that's a different matter. In transactions, friction can happen. But if the moment I walk into the room, by just looking at your face I'm having problems – this is a different level of problem, isn't it? If I am identified with my nation or religion or race or whatever, the moment I step into this room, before I meet you, before I really have a chance to have trouble with you, I already have a problem. [*Laughs*] This is because we are identified with something very limited.

Please look at this very carefully: whatever you identify with, your intellect will strive very hard to protect that identity, always. And your intellect is like a knife – it cuts. Whether you physically pull out a knife and stab somebody, or you poke people with your intellect, it could equally hurt, isn't it so?

Audience: Yes.

Sadhguru: Can you hurt somebody just with your thought, your emotion, your idea, with your words and whatever else? Just the way you look at them, you can hurt them. So, intellect is essentially a cutting instrument – a sharp instrument, because you said you want it sharp. I hope you kept it sharp. Otherwise it doesn't work. So, young people, it's very important, that if you cannot imagine a cosmic identity, at least a global identity is a must for you. Otherwise, being empowered by education, you will be the source of future disasters. Yes.

See, I want you to understand this. Why is it that all the cutting-edge technology first goes into military use? National identity, isn't it? The most powerful tools in the world are all designed as to how to eliminate you one day. So our brains are working to protect our identity all the time. Well, I don't want to get into any political stuff, but the wall* may be a more blatant manifestation of that. Essentially, it's limited identity, isn't it? Why is it that I wouldn't like to kill my own child, but if you are walking on the street, to get ten dollars out of your pocket, I will slash you? Because you're not mine, isn't it? My identity is only with this [*gestures a small circle near him*], not with that [*gestures far away*].

All of you are in premier institutions getting empowered with education. Education is an empowerment. Compared to what you could do without education, maybe you will do a hundred times more with education. When you have such a possibility, it is very important your identity is not a limited identity; at least identify with the planet and all the life on this planet if you can't think of cosmic. [*Applause*]

Alexander: Thank you for that answer.

Sadhguru: I'm sorry, I was referring to the Italians… just…

Alexander: [*Laughs*] No… I think you've touched on a lot of things that are quite pressing for us at Columbia, in the US, in the world at large. I mean, you went around the issue, but I think I'll kind of bring it in. Politics in America… we're more and more divided than before and quite polarized. This is

---

* Referring to the planned border wall between the US and Mexico.

something that troubles me. As someone in this community that has some less than popular opinions sometimes, I'm conscious of how I'm received, because of people who are passionate about these identities that their intellects defend, to use your words. How can I and others that share my desire bring people together in a divided world, divided community, even a divided street? How can we be individual actors to get people to focus on everything you just said, what we have in common and not what sets us apart?

Sadhguru: To address any situation, first of all we must face the situation as it is. Now you're saying it is getting more and more divided – I don't think so. I think it always was divided. Well, many of us face it. I face it. Every time I come to the immigration, you should see the way they address me, just looking at my face.

Adrianna: Does that make you angry?

Sadhguru: No, when somebody acts stupid, why will I get angry? [*Applause*] When somebody is exhibiting how small they are – compassion, not anger, isn't it? If I am in a bad mood – pity. If I am in a good mood – compassion. [*Laughter*]

Anger is another thing, because you're just showing how small an egg you are. You're still an egg; you have not hatched, that's all I'm saying. So, you must understand, very deep-rooted divides have always existed in this society. You don't want to face it. You've been glossing over it for a long time. I'm sure you're not naive enough to believe that in just two and a half years of your celebrity president, suddenly the country has become divided. Come on! It always was divided. Now the language has reached the top. Yes or no?

Audience: Yes.

Sadhguru: It's just that the language is coming to the surface. I think it better come to the surface than just boil inside forever. At least let everybody face it – this is what we are.

Let me tell you… I come to the immigration, I follow all the rules. I have a global entry, all right? [*Laughs*] You know, constantly I'm under all kinds of bright lights, and these fluorescent lights kind of irritate me. So I wear my shades. After I've crossed the immigration, when I come to the baggage claim area – you know, this has not happened once, this has happened a few times – they ask me to take my glasses off.

I said, "Why?"

They said, "You want to come to my office?"

What the hell are you trying to enforce on me? There are many others, white Americans, walking around with glasses. You don't ask them to take it off.

This is today. In twenty-first century. But you don't believe it. You think you are a just and fair society, but suddenly because of a new president something has happened.

You may not face it because of the color of your skin, but many of us are facing it. Yes. In some of these golf clubs and stuff – I can play better than them, but if I walk in there and say "hello", they'll just look through me. Somebody could be hurt by this, but I'm not that kind. I just see it's their pathetic condition of mind that they are like that. It doesn't bother me. But suppose I'm seeking a job or I want to do something else, I'm sure they would make sure that things don't work for me. Yes or no?

So this is not a new happening. It's been there. Maybe slowly things are changing, but I think it's good it's coming to the surface. It's up in your face, you're facing it, you're embarrassed by it. That is the first step to transformation. [*Laughs*] Am I saying something wrong? [*Applause*]

Varud: First step to transformation is now it's out in the world. We see it. You know, in India also we have divisions at an all-time high. What's now that second step that we can take as individuals going into the society to improve?

Sadhguru: See, you're saying that even in India it's at an all-time high. It's not at an all-time high. It is just people and media playing it up at a certain level. In a democratic society, there should be a free press. Unfortunately, all media across the world is owned by some corporation or the other. It is no more free. It is tangled up with money, big time. Largely, dedicated journalists are not there. They're all serving a company. Yes or no? It is time we produce some journalists, because media is not just another profession in a democratic society; it is an important pillar of democracy. Yes? Without it, a democracy will slowly go away and turn into something else. Because democracy means every four years or five years, depending on what's the term, a new set of people are going to rule the nation. It could be a complete mess if there are no checks and balances of various kinds. These are all going away because people have taken sides beforehand.

Today, you know in America – and in India also these days we know now – which media belongs to which party. Everybody knows. You can't call it media anymore. Media means they will report what is there. They can give a commentary about something, but essentially their business is to throw the facts at us. It's for us to form our opinions about facts that come to us. But today, don't you already know which media belongs to which party?

When this is the condition, you will hear a lot of things. And there is social media, anonymous journalists who don't dare to put their names on what they're saying. They are saying all kinds of things. But if you walk through the country and see, whether it's India or here, it is just the same as it was. There are problems and there are solutions. Both are happening, isn't it? So, if you go off television and switch off your phone and walk on the street, you will see everything is quite fine. [*Applause*]

Alexander: I just have one more follow-up question for young future business leaders in this room... we are at the very center of business.

Sadhguru: Why are you ignoring me?

Alexander: Oh, yeah. Well, you're a fashion icon, a Guru, and more. We don't want to limit you just as a business leader. And, you have a great throw of a frisbee in the video*. [*Laughs*] But what role can we play when people aren't as enlightened as, I guess, the people in this room, and can't really make the same connections as you? We are people that want to make a difference and are willing to have the courage – or, I guess, have compassion or pity depending on the mood we're in [*Laughs*] – so how do we do this? Because I think that's something that I genuinely want to play a big role in. I would like my life's purpose to have something to do with that.

---

* Referring to the introductory video about Sadhguru shown to the audience before the talk.

Sadhguru: See, I'm sure in your own little ways within the university, you're bringing some sense of equality and some sense of acceptance for all sorts of people. At the same time, do not make this about becoming a missionary for something, because then, without knowing what's happening to you, one day you will be totally skewed. Once you take on something with missionary zeal, you will see, you will get so badly identified with it and you yourself will become a source of the problem.

I'll share this with you. When I was just thirteen, fourteen years of age, I almost got into an armed struggle. This was the time when Che Guevara was our big brother and we were thinking of an armed struggle. We thought that was the only way to find solutions for India.

I saw the teachers espousing this openly in schools and professors talking about it in colleges, about how we all should join the armed struggle. There was a particular professor who had a sway on a few of us, and both his son and his daughter, who were twins, were my classmates. We were all ready. Actually, in another three to four days we were supposed to leave for the jungles of Andhra Pradesh to go fight.

Then I said to the son (his name was Ajay), "Hey, so we all are going. What are we taking?"

He said, "No, I'm not coming."

I said, "Why?"

"My father doesn't want me to go."

So, he wants us to go, but he doesn't want his son to go. [*Laughter*] Then, I sat back and thought what this is about.

We were all in the revolution and, okay, the girl was not going because only the boys were going. But at least this boy was supposed to go. He was just my age, in my class. But suddenly, his father said, "No, you cannot go because you can't die there. These idiots must die." Then actually I stepped back. I participated in various activities mildly bordering on revolution – sticking posters, giving out stuff, writing very strongly about what we thought was justice. But, actually when I look back and see, it was so juvenile and unjust by itself. At that time it looked like justice.

I know this is a delicate thing to say in America, but I want you to look at this with absolute openness – the moment we speak about justice, unknowingly, we will talk about revenge. Slowly, we will just slip into that. So, is justice needed? Absolutely. But the moment you start talking about it… it's like freedom. The moment you say "freedom", you'll start doing freaky things. Freedom is a consequence. So is justice. Justice is a consequence of a mature society. Justice is not a cause that you take up. The moment you take it up as a cause, you will see divisions of "you versus me" will happen. Once "you versus me" happens, even for the right reasons, all the wrong things will happen. Suppose in the name of justice, in this hall, two segments of the student body get divided. Even if it's for the right reason, the result will be all the wrong things, isn't it?

So, it's very important that we understand what is the cause and what is the consequence. Injustice is a consequence of an immature society. Injustice is a consequence of the limited identities people have taken in so many different ways. If you do not take that away and try to bring justice, all you will create is a full-on fight. And when a fight happens, there will be no justice of any kind. All that will happen is pain and destruction for all sorts of people.

I know this, because I was so fired up for those few years, I thought I'll go join the fight. Two of my friends went. One, I don't know where he disappeared. The other one became a major revolutionary leader in Karnataka, and he got killed by the police about eight years ago. His family informed me about this... you know, that boy was so dear to me. He was just one year younger to me.

Why I'm saying this is, the moment you speak about consequence as a cause, you're creating trouble, unknowingly. You will create more damage than solution. See, why does injustice happen? Why would I be unjust to you? Simply because my identity and my commitment to well-being is about myself, and maybe my family and community, not for you! It's already set. It's only a question of time when you and I come in touch and this prejudice will find expression. But it is set in my heart, isn't it so? Instead of working at what is happening within the human beings, which will take a lifelong commitment to solve, today we can go out on the street and shout, "Justice for everybody, justice for everybody!" All you need is a placard, shout for one day and go back home. Don't do that.

Don't talk about freedom, talk about responsibility. If we live responsibly, we will have a free society, isn't it? If we talk about freedom, we will do freaky things. I come from that era where next to revolution was freedom. We grew up in the sixties. "Freedom, freedom, freedom" – all that happened was that by the time I became thirty-five, at least twelve to thirteen of my very close friends died, either on motorcycles or because of overdoses. Yes, because of "freedom". So, freedom, justice, equality are all consequences of evolving a human being to a certain level of maturity. If you are not willing to do that work on an individual level, these things will only cause more trouble. [*Applause*]

Adrianna: I think it's a very related question but really targeted towards organized religion. I grew up Catholic. Its view and limited acceptance of the LGBTQ community is something that I've struggled with. The fact that I am LGBTQ and trying to understand how I fit in, oftentimes I was not accepted. It depended on, you know, how progressive a church was. But how do you see religion playing a role in the justice for being more tolerable and compassionate towards people from different sexualities?

Sadhguru: A bishop went to the mental asylum, not as a patient but to give a talk. So they gathered people like here. He spoke. Nobody was listening to what he was saying; they were all busy with their own things. But there was just one guy in the front row who, without batting an eyelid, was listening to and drinking up every word the bishop was saying. Nobody else, not a single person, was listening except this one guy. After an hour-long speech, the moment it got over, that guy got up, went to a medical professional who was in the hall, said something to him, and left.

The bishop was very eager to know what that guy said, because he was the only guy listening to him. The bishop enquired with the doctor, "What did that guy say? He was listening to me very keenly."

The doctor said, "He just asked, 'Why am I in, and why is he out?'" [*Laughter*]

Alexander: As a follow-up, what are your thoughts on human sexuality?

Sadhguru: Oh, I didn't think about it, but I was born out of it. I'm a consequence.

Adrianna: But one thing that you've mentioned previously in one of your talks is that sexuality shouldn't be promoted. I almost felt as though you meant don't publicize your gayness or your non-gayness. So, I'm trying to understand why you said that…

Sadhguru: I thought this is one aspect of life which doesn't need publicity. Anyway, people will go for it, it doesn't need any marketing. If you want to sell a drink, you have to market it; if you make a movie, you have to market it; if you write a book, you have to market it. Sexuality does not need marketing. It's been on for a million years without any marketing. So, I said, "Why are you publicizing it?" Everybody will do what they have to do. What individual people do with their bodies is their business. It's not a public debate. [*Applause*]

Varud: So, I think we're about to wrap up our questions, and we're going to open up questions to the audience. Before we get there, my favorite topic, food. [*Laughs*] You cook, yourself. I believe Isha has also published a cookbook.

Sadhguru: Mmhmm [*indicating agreement*].

Varud: Can you talk a little bit about food from the Yogic diet perspective? Or what are the things that we should be actively doing on a daily basis if I do choose to go the less sinful route one day, in terms of gluttony, when it comes to food? What are the tenets of the diet that we would be looking at? And, if you have a favorite recipe to share?

Sadhguru: Right now, we are running two good restaurants. And another three to four okay restaurants... because I am also a food buff, not for eating, but for cooking. [*Laughs*] Don't get much time these days, but at least my daughter certifies that I'm the best cook in the world. So, she can't be wrong.

We are Telugu families who at one time came from Andhra Pradesh and moved into Karnataka, a particular kind of region where spice is available in a hundred different forms. Our families were initially martial families that later became business families. Those days, when the men went to war and out of the country for business, there was no text and email. The only way the women could get their men back was by holding them by the tongue – it's the taste of the food.

I'm talking a couple of centuries ago, they were going out to places like Burma and Japan, and had no reason to come back. It was not like today, where you hop onto a plane and are back in a few hours. It was months of journey. You're kind of tired, so what's going to bring you back? It's the taste of food. Wherever you go, this spice was just eating you up. [*Laughs*] So they always came back. The women said, "We hold them by their tongues; you can't hold these idiots any other way." So a lot of culinary expertise, enormous mastery over these things. I picked up a little bit. With that I prepared a menu for this restaurant. Today, it is rated as the second-best vegetarian restaurant in Asia. [*Applause*] If you happen to be in Chennai or Hyderabad, you must go and eat there.

How to extract out of this planet things which cause enormous pleasure? Cooking is an important part of this. But when you don't know anything else, the simple way is to numb all your senses and just get smoked up. One weed will do. But to prepare this meal, you have to go out into the garden or the jungle and pick specific things. This was normal – people would go out into the fields, picking that specific thing for today's cooking. This kind of care was there. Today, that kind of care is difficult because we're just on the run, everything is on the fly. So, we've not done much at the restaurant, but still it's hugely appreciated. The moment people come in touch with it, that care is there.

What kind of food? There are two parts to the food. One is… after all, it's fuel for this body, so it's important that it fits into the system well. Another thing is, it has to pass through the tongue. So, we don't have to gulp it down. We want to enjoy it. When you're really hungry, anything goes, isn't it? It's a question of survival. Let's say you've not eaten for five days, whatever edible thing comes your way is great. But most of the people on this planet have passed that stage; survival is pretty well taken care of. Now, culinary delights become very significant. See, my mouth is watering, because I'm thinking of my own cooking. [*Laughs*] I have not looked at your book yet.

These are two different aspects, but the first is most fundamental. Let's understand this. Food is not a religion, not a philosophy, and should not become an ideology. It is just fuel for this body. The whole thing is: in what form and in what composition will it provide this body the best nourishment with least amount of trouble?

None of you are biology students, are you? No, just business. In the animal kingdom, you can largely divide animals either as herbivores and carnivores. There are, of course, mixed or omnivorous animals, but largely it is herbivores and carnivores. If you look at the basic physical structure of these two kinds of creatures, you will see there's a fundamental difference in the way their bodies are constructed, particularly the digestive system. From the lip to the anal outlet, digestion is happening at various different levels. This is known as the alimentary canal.

To start with, the jaws and mouth structure. If you have not seen tigers or lions, you must have noticed this if you have a dog or a cat – all carnivorous animals have only cutting action in their jaw movement. Yes? All the herbivores have cutting and grinding action. What do you have? You have both cutting and grinding action. Why is this so? Because there are certain enzymes in your saliva; digestion begins for you in your mouth, not in your stomach. The more the food stays in your mouth, the better your digestive process is.

Now that you asked for the Yogic perspective, there are some systems of Yoga that say you must chew every mouthful twenty-four times. I don't go by these things; I want people to decide how much to chew by the texture of the food. But if you don't know how to chew, they say to chew it twenty-four times. If you do that, at least thirty to forty percent of the digestion will happen in your mouth itself. Now, food is primed well in your mouth; that is what the stomach is expecting – half-digested food – so that the rest of it can be done quickly.

If you take any carbohydrate or grain, let's say a grain of rice, and keep it in your mouth, you will see that within thirty to forty seconds it will turn sweet, because the carbohydrate is turning into sugar right there. But today, most people are just gulping things down. So you're not using this part of the digestive system at all. Everything is on the stomach, and it is being overloaded. It's not an accident that fifty percent of the world's antacids are consumed in the United States of America. Three hundred million people are consuming fifty percent of the world's antacids. This is a clear statement on the food that you're eating. Obviously, you are eating the completely wrong kind of food.

So if you look at the incisors and molars in carnivorous and herbivorous animals, you can see that your structure is like that of an herbivore.

The length of the alimentary canal in a carnivorous animal could be anywhere between three to four times the length of its body. In all the herbivores, it's five to six times the length of their body. If you look at your own alimentary canal, it is anywhere between twenty-four to thirty feet; this means it is five to six times the length of your body. Why this is so is… let's say you eat raw meat, it will take anywhere between seventy to seventy-four hours for it to go through your system. If you eat cooked meat – if you are having it rare, that's a different matter – if you cook it well and eat it, then it will take anywhere between fifty to fifty-six hours to go through the system. If you cook vegetables and eat them, it will take anywhere between twenty to thirty hours to go through the system – depending on the type of vegetable, how much fiber it has and other things. If you eat a raw vegetable, it will take anywhere between twelve to fifteen hours to go through the system. If you eat a fruit, it will take one and a half to three hours to go through the system.

Any food which stays in your body for long periods of time means excessive bacteria in the system. You spend a lot of energy just to fight them down. In Ayurveda, in the Eastern systems of medicine, whatever problem you go to them with, the first thing is they'll purge you, because a clean colon is a symbol of health. But the moment you eat certain types of food, your colon can never be clean. So there are problems today. The amount of colon cancer and intestinal cancer is so high.

One thing is people are eating food that is not suitable for the system. Another thing is they're eating old food. If I walk into any store, what I see is that any food you want to buy is at least a month or two months old. Fortunately, in India, except in big cities, still if we want to buy a vegetable, it must be plucked that morning. It is plucked at six or six-thirty in the morning, and we cook at eight-thirty or nine. We want to eat it when the vegetable is still alive, and it will make a world of difference. Today people are talking about farmers market, organic stores and the works, but this is how the world lived thirty, forty years ago – before you business guys totally messed it up! [*Laughter*]

I know all this is not possible for everybody to maintain. Don't go by what I say – don't listen to anybody when it comes to food. Just learn to listen to your body, with what kind of food your body is most comfortable. Not your mind, not your tongue – your body should feel very comfortable. If your body is comfortable, one thing is it'll bring down your sleep quota. If your lethargy goes down, if your sleep goes down, your agility goes up, your alertness goes up; this means the body is happy with the food that you're consuming. After eating the food, if the condition of the body is such that unless you drink something caffeinated or sugar loaded, you cannot get up and do your work, then this food is not good for you; you should not be touching that.

I would say, instead of going by all kinds of prescriptions, there are simple ways to become alert to the food. We cannot do it here, but we could teach you how. If something appears on your plate, you must know whether it will go well with you or not. It's happened to me, sometimes, where the food has been laced with some poison. If it comes before me, I just look at it and say, "I'm not eating this. This is not good. Something is wrong with it, seriously." This is simply because your body is capable of that. You just throw something to a dog – not your pet dog because he's become like you [*Laughter*] – a dog which is free. In Brooklyn, are there still some free dogs?

Alexander: Hipster dogs that's got moustaches… [*Laughter*]

Sadhguru: If you throw something to him, one sniff, he knows whether to eat it or not, isn't it? How come you don't know? You know, in the evolutionary scale, you have the most sensitive neurological system. If you look at the food, you must know how this food will behave within you. Based on that, you, the business people, can shape the markets of tomorrow. [*Applause*]

Adrianna: So on the note of what we're consuming and putting in our bodies, one of the things that I'd like to know the truth about is the increase in addiction in the US. It's something that has personally really touched a lot of the loved ones in my family and friends, and I see it as a growing trend amongst my generation and younger generations who are using it as a coping mechanism. Why do you think people are looking to drugs to solve their problems, and what is an organic way for them to solve that?

Sadhguru: It is a natural process of graduation. Last generation went on alcohol. This generation is upping it a little bit. They don't want to do the same damn thing, but a bigger dose. There was a time when alcohol was illegal in this country, you know? It went wild, bootlegging. You know, our center is in Tennessee. So bootlegging or moonshining, whatever you want to call it, went out of control. Then the government decided it's better to put a tax on alcohol and make money, which they did. Now they decided it's better to tax marijuana and make money. Believe me, watch my words, in another twenty-five years cocaine will be legal. Why not? In India also, there are students campaigning, "Why can't we make marijuana legal!"

This generation does not know that in Nepal, Bhutan and the northeastern states of India, marijuana grows in whole valleys. Nobody ever bothers to touch it. A few people who have nothing to do in their life smoke themselves up. Rest will not touch it because it's all over the place. I've trekked extensively in the Himalayas. We're just walking through hash plants, chest-high. If you just brush your hands through it, it'll stick to your hand, you can roll it up and you can smoke. Some of you are looking dreamy – "Oh, this is the place to go." [*Laughter*] But now, we are suddenly making this into a big thing.

Students were asking me, "Why can't we make marijuana legal in India?" I said that it was never illegal till the American government insisted on destroying all the hemp crops in the 1960s. Hemp was a very important textile in India, but they couldn't make out the difference between hemp and marijuana. Though they are same species, they are of a different kind – hemp grows up to fifteen feet, marijuana grows just about five to six feet tall. They thought it was all coming from the hemp farms and said, "No, you have to destroy it." Hemp was hugely cultivated, but they burned down all the hemp farms. So, all the marijuana moved to Afghanistan. [*Laughs*]

Right now, I don't know what terms you use – it's called "smoked up". You're using the same terms?

Audience: High!

Sadhguru: High. In India it's "smoked up". "Smoke" is just cigarette; "smoked up" is the weed. We have nothing against anything. It is just that a human being is always trying to enhance his or her life all the time. How do you enhance your life? Some foolish people believe by acquiring things they will enhance their life. But, even if you live in a palace, you could be miserable. Yes? Enhancement of life will happen only by heightening your faculties. So I asked, "Suppose you want to fly in a small plane and you find the pilot is smoked up, you want to fly with him?"

"Hmm," they said.

Then I said, "Okay, you're not getting the point. You need a serious surgery. Then the surgeon comes and he's smoked up. You want the surgery?"

They said, "No."

So you understand that with lowered faculties he will not make a good pilot or a good surgeon. Then how come you believe you will make a great student? [*Applause*]

Alexander: Changing gears slightly, I have a question submitted by "The Prolific Anonymous". How do you decide between your principles, goals and priorities versus the person you like the most? The goals and principles both come from the same mind or heart.

Sadhguru: Well, it depends what you have taken up. If your goal is just to earn a certain amount of money or comfort for somebody who matters to you, you should be willing to drop those silly things. But if your goal is such that it is not about your comfort, it is not about your money, but it's a larger goal for the well-being of the people, then you don't have to take a decision. Decisions will happen. They will just happen. You don't have to decide.

Varud: So I think we have about thirty minutes to take audience questions.

Radha: Namaskar, Sadhguru. My name is Radha Kulkarni. I'm a Columbia alum and studied policy here, not business. [*Laughs*] And I work at the United Nations now. Your talks are both inspiring and grounding at the same time, and that's a difficult balance. So thank you so much for coming to Columbia and speaking with us. Much appreciated.

My question to you, Sadhguru, is that there's so much suffering in the world, like when I travel on work or otherwise, I observe that on the one hand there is lack of even basic peace – there's so much violence. And on the other hand, there is lack of even basic resources, and abject poverty. So I would be curious to hear your perspective on why every single person has such different starting points in life. A child based in Africa, who doesn't even have water and perhaps will die of malnutrition, has a very different starting point than a billionaire's child who is perhaps sitting somewhere in the middle of North America. So why this disparity? And how and where does it sit in the larger scheme of things or in the cycle of the cosmos or life, if

that's how we call it? And also, that gets me to the question of
"Who are we?".

Sadhguru: Ah! That's a very Indian question. [*Laughter*] I must
tell you this because you're also working at the UN. You know,
every year we trek in Tibet. Three years ago, there were people
from over forty countries trekking with me. So, one Indian
person who lives in the United States stood up to ask a question,
and the question went on for over eight minutes. You've been
very brief. [*Laughs*] So, the question was going on, and for this
international audience, their heads were spinning because they
could not grasp the question. Then I said, "Please relax, this is
an Indian question." Because we have practiced asking questions
for over 10,000 to 12,000 years. This is a nation where even
when so-called divine entities came, they could not give us any
commandments because all we had were questions. [*Laughter*]
Relentless questioning.

Then, one Chinese lady, who was working in the United
Nations for more than thirty years, said, "Sadhguru, even in
those thirty years when I worked in the United Nations, only
Indians asked questions."

Anyway, so why is there disparity? I thought you know the
answer. There is disparity because those who have don't care
about those who don't have. It's very simple. Those who have
want to take more and more; those who don't have, just don't
have. There are various aspects. It's found expression in many
different ways. It started with imperialism and, even now,
every nation is seeing how to take the maximum resource from
everywhere else, isn't it? So, we know the source of the problem;
the question is, what is the solution? Some studies have said that

in 2016, we produced enough food for ten billion people, but we were only 7.1 billion people then. Still, thirty-five percent of the planet is malnourished.

You know the statistics better than me; you're in the United Nations. When we are producing much more food than we actually need for the population, still one third of the population is starving. Millions of children die of malnourishment all over – not just in Africa, even in India. India has the highest malnourished population right now.

Largely our identities are still biological. If you say "my race", it's biology; if you say "my family", it's biology, isn't it? When you are biological, you're set within a small boundary and your instinct of self-preservation is at its highest. In your intelligence or in your brain structure, there is something known as the reptilian brain that is approximately the size of your fist. That is still working like a reptile, fixing boundaries all the time and trying to protect those boundaries, which finds expression in so many different ways.

But there's another dimension of intelligence which is the cerebral cortex that makes you a human being who thinks about and struggles with these issues. If you were a tiger, you wouldn't care that a goat's child is hungry because, after all, it's your food. Once you become a human being, you actually don't care, but still one part of you, which makes you human, makes you struggle. You need to empower that. As humanity, our instinct of self-preservation must go down, and we need to empower the longing to expand, which is always there within us. Today it is finding expression as ambition, conquest, or maybe, simply shopping.

What is this all about?

You want to be something more than what you are right now, isn't it? Now the question is, if you become something more today, are you fully settled tomorrow? No, you want to be something more and something more. So, you seem to be going towards some kind of goal in installments. How much more will settle you for good? What do you think? Suppose I make you the queen of this planet, will you be fulfilled? I am asking you. Don't look at me hopefully, I will not commit such a blunder. [*Laughter*] But suppose we put a throne on the North Pole and make you sit there as the queen of the planet, would you be fulfilled? No, you will look at the stars, you will look at the galaxies. This is the nature of the human being, because there is something in this human being that doesn't like boundaries and wants to expand limitlessly. You want to expand but you want to do it in small measure, as if you're going to live here for a million years.

All you business students must move from your personal ambition to a larger vision. Ambition means constipated expression of growth. Vision means seamless expression of growth. This must happen to you. How much should you grow? You should not determine this. You must gas yourself fully, make yourself competent, and enhance your competence. Let's see how far it goes. Yes? Why should you fix the limit? Whatever limits and goals you set are just an exaggeration of what little you know today, isn't it so? Today what little you know, you're exaggerating it and thinking this is ambition. Being in the United Nations, you have much knowledge about many things, but even if you have studied the libraries on this planet, all your knowledge is minuscule compared to what this cosmic space is, isn't it? If you identify with this minuscule knowledge that you have, you will become a minuscule; because you're such a minuscule, you will feel endlessly insecure about anything and everything that's happening to you.

See, he [*Alexander*] lives in Brooklyn; still nobody stabbed him. What are you insecure about? In Yoga, we have another system. We call this the intelligence of ignorance. We always identify with our ignorance because our knowledge is so small. Our ignorance is boundless. What we do not know is boundless, isn't it? What we know is so little. So, identify with what you do not know, then your life will expand rapidly. Your intelligence will stay alert through your life. If you identify with knowledge, your intelligence will sleep and you will make a fool of yourself with a big degree. Yes.

If your human intelligence is on, it is very natural to be inclusive. If your reptilian brain is on, it is very natural to be exclusive, to put up walls. So as a human society, as nations, we have put up walls and walls for everything, isn't it? The very damn marketplace is a big wall. It's a Wall Street, all right. [*Laughter*] The markets and industries are controlled so that everybody does not thrive. Yes or no? Anyway, you didn't ask me what happened to this food that we grow for ten billion people. You must find out; you're in the UN. All of you must find out why we produce much more food than what we need and still one-third of humanity is starving. Shouldn't your humanity want to find out? Please, you must find out. [*Applause*]

Prem: Thank you so much for having this event. My name is Prem, I'm a sophomore studying history. My question is about this idea of cosmic or global identity. I think it's no secret that many of us here, no matter where we came from before this, now have a certain level of privilege of being at a place like Columbia. And I think I'm confused as to whether this notion of a global or cosmic identity is predicated on a sense of privilege, and that certain people in this world don't actually have a privilege of being able to live beyond their most immediate surroundings because of discrimination, racism, sexism, and so on. How can we, as people that maybe do have more privilege, leverage that to make that global identity mean something more than just us talking about it here?

Sadhguru: This happened in Columbia University. Two young ladies met. One of them said, "I will not marry till I turn thirty." Another said, "Well, I'm married, but I will never turn thirty." [*Laughs*] So we must understand the investment in problems that people have made. When your problems are my business, I don't want your problems to go away. I was at the World Economic Forum at Davos and there was a big thing going on about Sudan. American celebrities were posing with this starved out child. Photographs everywhere and compassion. I appreciate the intention, I'm not against it. Everybody has to do it in their own way. But in the same video, they were showing all these militants taking automatic weapons, and death everywhere, and massive large-scale rape. It's almost like if you're a man, you will die; if you're a woman, you get raped. Southern Sudan was like that some time ago. Now it's coming to some kind of sense. So, dozens of these guys were just shooting in the sky.

I said, "See, these guys are not shooting at somebody. They're shooting in the sky. That means they have limitless supply of armaments. You can't take away the guns from them but the bullets you can. I know what gun they're using. I know what caliber it is. There are just eight companies which are making these bullets, armaments. Six of them are in the United States. I'll give you the addresses – all you have to do is lock these down. In about six months' time when they run out of bullets, they will have to hack people and at least the number of people killed will go down. Once they don't have bullets, other people will know how to deal with them.

I'm saying when my trouble is your business, will you give it up? So, as young people who are going into the business world, don't think you have to go there as a victim of what is existing right now. I'm not trying to blame everybody – this is how we've shaped it and all of us are responsible for this. Till now, this is how we've done business. It is time to change it. And in the last twenty years, there's been a lot of commentary about me in the social media – "Why is he always with corporate leaders? Oh, he has become corrupt. He's moving with this person, that person." Because I see that if you want to change the world today, how we do business has to change. It is not the success of the military or politics which makes a nation; it is the success of business which makes a nation. So how we are conducting our business is important. If you don't transform the business leaders, how the hell are you going to change anything?

At the World Economic Forum, somebody important asked me, "Sadhguru, if we have to do one thing for you to transform this world, what is it?"

I said, "Just give me twenty-five people for five days. I will change the world in the next two to three years."

They asked, "Who are these twenty-five people?"

I named the top twenty-five leaders of the top twenty-five nations in the world. I said, "Normally, with ordinary people, two and a half days are enough to transform them. But these are politicians, so five days. I'm just taking insurance." [*Laughs*] Even if there's a ten percent change in the way that they are looking at the world, if they become ten percent more inclusive, the world will change dramatically, believe me. One thing is we don't have to exploit the planet so badly to make food for ten billion people to feed seven billion people, and that too, one-third of them going hungry. This can be solved if these twenty-five people make up their minds.

Today, you're sitting here in the university as a student, but tomorrow you'll be part of a larger company. Well, when you join up, you may not be able to decide how to run this company. But don't become a victim and give up. In India, when we say "Yoga", we always use the lotus flower as a symbolism. This is true with every flower but particularly with the lotus: the more stinky the slush is, the more fragrant and beautiful the lotus flower becomes. So we always use this analogy for the way a Yogi should be. When you see filth, you can become allergic to it and become an ascetic if you wish. Or you can say, "Everywhere is filth, so let me also become filth." A lot of people become this. Or another way is you transform the filth into a flower. This choice you have. Wherever you are, whatever role you play, you have this choice. Make sure you're always a part of the solution, not a part of the problem. Do this one thing, and depending upon your competence, let's see how far you go. [*Applause*]

Questioner: So Sadhguru, thank you for being here. What advice would you give someone with healing gifts, someone who can help people create miracles in their lives, to grow in service to the world?

Sadhguru: A miracle means – everybody walks on the floor, you walk on the ceiling. Everybody swims in the water, but you walk upon the water. Please don't do these things. If you walk upon the water, where the hell will you swim? It's important that you don't do unreasonable things. Right now, maybe you're thinking we are sitting in Columbia University, but we are sitting here in this universe. We don't know where the thing begins and where it ends. We do not know its nature. And the damn planet is round and spinning, and we're sitting here and talking all this. Isn't it a miracle? Just pay attention and tell me one thing that's not a miracle out here. What was soil that you walked upon yesterday, is a flower today. What was yesterday's soil is the food on your plate today. Yes? He agrees with me [*pointing to Varud*].

Varud: Good. We're good.

Sadhguru: Isn't this all a miracle? So, there is no need for you to do something unreasonable. Miracles are just happening everywhere. You are a miracle, isn't it? Somebody gave you two cells – see how you've become. [*Laughs*] Isn't this a miracle? Those who have no eyes for life, who are too engrossed within themselves, think they will perform miracles. Let's say, 500 years ago, I pulled out something from my pocket and started speaking to somebody in India. If I said I am the messenger or the son or himself, would you believe it or no? What is one person's magic is another person's engineering. So, this is why we're talking about inner engineering, where you can live magically, which is very important. Isn't everything about this life magical? But unfortunately, most human beings are not experiencing it. They are muddled with their own logic and stuck in it so badly they do not feel and enjoy the magic of their existence.

The significance of being human is just this… Just take a part of our system, let's say your eyes. Even now there are certain fish in the oceans whose skin became photosensitive, they can sense what is light, what is darkness – that is their level of seeing. From there, our visual apparatus has developed to this point where our eyes, our brains, our neurological system, are at the highest level of development that's happened on this planet. So, our experience of life is capable of being magical. For all those of you who are trying to do magic by snorting or smoking or something… let me tell you, a little magic does happen there also – I'm not somebody to look at this as a moral issue. It is just that it's destroying the possibilities. That's the only concern.

Isn't this human mechanism the most sophisticated chemical factory on this planet? Because you're all business guys, the question is only, are you a great CEO or a lousy CEO? That's all. If you are a great CEO, you will get what you want out of this. If you're a lousy CEO, you get tension, anxiety, misery. I get ecstasy. Thank you. [*Applause*]

Mathan: Sadhguru, thank you for being here. My name is Mathan. I'm a first-year MBA student. My question is actually also about identity. You've spoken about the need or the benefit of detaching from a biological identity. And this question kind of came up again and again. I'm curious, if somebody wants to act positively in society, there's an instinct to start from the people that you identify with biologically. And since you've spoken about the need to detach from that identity, what's the alternative to starting from that biological community and… maybe I've understood you the wrong way, because I see you shaking your head?

Sadhguru: See, I did not ever say you should detach yourself from biological identity. Instead of seeing your mother, father, brother, sisters, and the larger family as your biological identity, why don't you see that they are the first people that you have access to? You can work most effectively only where you have access and acceptance, isn't it? People are always telling me, "Sadhguru, you must come and work in Africa."

I say, "No, I will not work in Africa." I would like somebody to give me at least five billion dollars before I enter Africa, because without that handholding you can't make a difference there. You cannot. You will go there and waste your life. Nothing will happen. I work in India not because of my nationality, but because in India if you give me ten dollars, I will make it into a thousand dollars in effect – I have access and acceptance with the people. But if I go to Africa, if you give me a hundred dollars, it will become one dollar, because there is no access and acceptance out there, and the problem there is of a completely different nature.

So, where you choose to work is not a question of your nationality or your ethnicity or your family. Where you have access and acceptance, that's where you must start; otherwise you will just waste your time and energy. Life is just a combination of time and energy, isn't it? Limited amount of time, limited amount of energy. If you run into walls here and there, time and energy will go, and your life will go. It's very important you run through the door, not into the wall. Yes? You go where there is openness; then if you want to turn around and go somewhere else, that's a different matter. But you must always start work where there is acceptance and access. Without access what will you do? You'll just beat your head on the wall. [*Applause*] And if you have a great idea, if you cannot even sell it to your family, you're not going to sell it to anybody. [*Laughs*]

Varud: Just the last thing we are going to close with for *Youth and Truth* is, what worries you the most about the youth of tomorrow?

Sadhguru: Oh, this nonsense where every generation is worried about the next generation – I'm not that kind. The previous generation was worried about me. They didn't know a thing about me, but they just worried about me. I'm not worrying about you. Because I know with all your madness, you'll figure out things as things go by. [*Applause*]

Being worried about the next generation has always been an ancient malady. You must see what Socrates was supposed to have said about the next generation. He said, "They have no respect, they don't stand up when elders come, they're not thinking straight, they're going to ruins." Well, 2000 years ago, the guy was saying the same thing. It's time to change that.

I'm not worried about you because I see, for the first time in the history of humanity, this generation is empowered in ways that nobody had imagined possible. Yes? Our survival is better organized than ever before, and if we want to change the world, no better time. I want you to recognize this because many great beings have come right from ancient times and every generation had their greats, but even if they raised their voices and spoke, hardly twenty-five people heard. Today, if you have something sensible to say, you can say it to the whole world! Do not underestimate that.

One thing you should do as business people and young people is clean up that space a little bit. All kinds of idiots are saying things loudly, and sane things are not really getting across. Yes? Social media, I feel, will mature probably in the next five to ten years. People will know how to filter it. But there is a concern because of the way we are using these technologies against ourselves and against everybody else. They are telling me seventy percent of the data is pornography. And they're telling me, on the internet, over 1.2 million children below fifteen years of age are being sold for all kinds of filthy things. I think, as a society, as human beings, when we start selling our children, that means we've hit the bottom. What do you think? We have really hit the bottom, isn't it? So, these are things that young people can change. How many in this campus?

Alexander: Five thousand.

Sadhguru: If 5000 people meet, if you get active, and you're determined to change the language and the direction of what's happening on the internet, believe me, you can do it. Just do it. Let's make it happen. [*Applause*]

AN UNEXPECTED GUEST

In March 2019, students of Columbia Business School began seeing images of a Guru-like figure on their social media feed and on several well-designed brochures on their college notice boards. While some ignored it and went about their business, others were intrigued. Columbia Business School had hosted a number of notable speakers on its campus, including some of the world's leading business leaders, CEOs and public figures such as Bill Gates, Warren Buffett, Carlos Brito, Henry Paulson, Ratan Tata, among others, but a Guru was least expected here, or so the students thought.

Though Sadhguru was well-known among the students of Asian origins – some knew him as a spiritual leader, some as an ecological activist, while others as the next YouTube sensation – they would soon encounter a very different facet of Sadhguru at their very own college campus.

MANHATTAN STUDENTS JAZZ IT UP!

It was Isha's New York volunteer Keerthi's first attempt at organizing an event for Sadhguru at an educational institution. Despite the lack of experience, the jigsaw pieces of the event came together. The setting was semi-formal, and the student-moderators were from varying backgrounds and had an interestingly diverse range of questions. "Just what we wanted it to be. In no time, things began to fall in place," shares Keerthi. "Though we were initially apprehensive about whether enough awareness was spread across the institute to fill up the venue, we were pleasantly surprised as registrations soon started pouring in. The response from the student community was quite impressive."

Naresh, a PhD student at Columbia, agrees: "As in most other *Youth and Truth* events in India and elsewhere, we had to block another venue for students who could not be accommodated in the auditorium so that they could watch the conversation live on screens."

Among several creative ideas floated by many to create awareness about the event, Naresh and his friends suggested bringing a jazz band to trigger intrigue and excitement. "We invited a group of jazz musicians from Manhattan School of Music and held a few sessions as a prelude to the main event. The band performed in the background as we distributed pamphlets to students who had gathered to enjoy the music," shares Naresh. "We also conducted quizzes and game shows around common questions and issues that are bothering students, and hinted that possible solutions to their deepest questions were soon coming their way."

While it was obvious that most Indian and other Asian students would turn up, Naresh and his team were focused on reaching out to students of other nationalities, especially those who were new to Sadhguru. He says, "There are students from over eighty nationalities on the campus, and our target was to have a representation from each as this was a unique opportunity which we didn't want them to miss." Soon, there was a palpable excitement in the air. Students started sending in their questions through various digital platforms. "We were surprised to meet many students who were keen to learn Yogic and meditative techniques from Sadhguru," he admits.

A BREATH OF FRESH AIR

On 29 April 2019, the students of Columbia Business School witnessed the moment they were keenly waiting for. "Sadhguru walked into the packed Uris Hall with folded hands, and greeted the students and faculty members," Keerthi says. Though a significant majority of the audience sat through the event out of sheer curiosity, not expecting anything in particular, they left impressed and profoundly enriched. "Sadhguru began with a greeting, and when very few reciprocated, he quipped whether we were already not on talking terms with him, which sent a bout of laughter in the auditorium and eased the atmosphere – creating the right ambience for a freewheeling conversation," Keerthi discloses.

"One of the most remarkable parts of the conversation between Sadhguru and student-moderators was Sadhguru's insights packed in humor," says Naresh. "Often, Sadhguru articulated his deepest wisdom in the lightest possible way, which not only made it palatable but also opened several rigid doors of my mind I was unaware of until then. It made me more curious about things beyond my limited identities of friends, career and family."

"Sadhguru offered a completely new perspective on the most pressing issues of our times, such as the effects of smoking marijuana, religious intolerance to the LGBTQ community, among several others. These issues are particularly relevant to the youth in this part of the world," shares a student who attended the event.

"I feel there is a strong dose of truth and clarity in every word that Sadhguru speaks, which makes him popular among all segments of the society, especially the youth. Moreover, his presence loosened some unnecessary protocols and etiquettes which I felt was the need of the hour at the school," another audience member observes.

Another attendee summarizes the impact the event had on him and many others: "Till date, I feel privileged to have sat in Sadhguru's presence and have breathed the same air as he does, for over two hours. I feel those two captivating hours healed something that was troubling me deep inside, and brought a breath of fresh air, not just in my life, but in that of many students on the campus."

ABOUT THE AUTHOR

Yogi, mystic and visionary, Sadhguru is a spiritual master with a difference. Absolute clarity of perception places him in a unique space, not only in matters spiritual but in business, environmental and international affairs, and opens a new door on all that he touches.

Ranked amongst the fifty most influential people in India, Sadhguru is known as a speaker and opinion maker of international renown. He has been conferred the Padma Vibhushan, India's highest annual civilian award, accorded for exceptional and distinguished service.

Sadhguru has initiated large-scale ecological initiatives, such as *Rally for Rivers* and *Cauvery Calling*, to revitalize India's severely depleted rivers. These projects have found phenomenal support among India's people and leadership. They are internationally accredited and recognized as game changers that can establish a blueprint for global economic development that is ecologically sustainable. In 2022, Sadhguru launched the *Conscious Planet - Save Soil Movement*, to raise awareness on the alarming rate of soil degradation and its dire consequences for all life, and to bring about the necessary government policy changes across the globe.

Sadhguru has been a primary speaker at the United Nations General Assembly and several other UN forums. He has also been regularly invited to speak at establishments such as the World Economic Forum, the World Bank, the House of Lords, the University of Oxford, MIT, Google and Microsoft, to name a few.

With a celebratory engagement with life on all levels, Sadhguru's areas of active involvement encompass fields as diverse as architecture and visual design, poetry and painting, aviation and driving, and sports and music. He is the designer of several unique buildings and consecrated spaces at the Isha Yoga Center, which have received wide attention for their combination of intense sacred power and strikingly innovative aesthetics.

Three decades ago, Sadhguru established the Isha Foundation, a non-profit human-service organization, with human well-being as its core commitment.

app.sadhguru.org
isha.sadhguru.org
facebook.com/sadhguru
twitter.com/SadhguruJV
youtube.com/Sadhguru
instagram.com/Sadhguru

rallyforrivers.org
cauverycalling.org
consciousplanet.org

ISHA FOUNDATION

Founded by Sadhguru, Isha Foundation is a non-profit human service organization, supported by over eleven million volunteers in over 300 centers worldwide. Recognizing the possibility of each person to empower another, Isha Foundation has created a massive movement that is dedicated to address all aspects of human well-being, without subscribing to any particular ideology, religion or race.

Isha's unique approach in cultivating human potential has gained worldwide recognition and reflects in the Foundation's special consultative status with the Economic and Social Council (ECOSOC) of the United Nations.

The Foundation is headquartered at the Isha Yoga Center, at the base of the Velliangiri Mountains in southern India, and at the Isha Institute of Inner-sciences on the spectacular Cumberland Plateau in central Tennessee, USA.

isha.sadhguru.org
facebook.com/ishafoundation
twitter.com/ishafoundation
youtube.com/ishafoundation
instagram.com/isha.foundation

ISHA YOGA CENTER

Isha Yoga Center, founded under the aegis of Isha Foundation, is located at the foothills of the Velliangiri Mountains. Envisioned and created by Sadhguru as a powerful *sthana* (a center for inner growth), this popular destination attracts people from all parts of the world. It is unique in its offering of all aspects of Yoga – *gnana* (knowledge), *karma* (action), *kriya* (energy), and *bhakti* (devotion) and revives the *Guru-shishya paramparya* (the traditional method of knowledge transfer from Master to disciple).

Isha Yoga Center provides a supportive environment for people to shift to healthier lifestyles, improve interpersonal relationships, seek a higher level of self-fulfilment, and realize their full potential.

The Center is located 30 km west of Coimbatore, a major industrial city in southern India which is well connected by air, rail and road. All major national airlines operate regular flights into Coimbatore from Chennai, Delhi, Mumbai and Bengaluru. Train services are available from all major cities in India. Regular bus and taxi services are also available from Coimbatore to the Center.

Visitors are advised to contact the Yoga Center for availability and reservation of accommodation well in advance, as it is generally heavily booked.

Learn more at:

isha.sadhguru.org/center/isha-yoga-center-coimbatore.

DHYANALINGA

The Dhyanalinga is a powerful and unique energy form created by Sadhguru from the essence of Yogic sciences. Situated at the Isha Yoga Center, it is the first of its kind to be completed in over 2000 years. The Dhyanalinga is a meditative space that does not subscribe to any particular faith or belief system, nor does it require any ritual, prayer, or worship.

The Dhyanalinga was consecrated by Sadhguru after three years of an intense process of *prana pratishtha*. Housed within an architecturally striking pillarless dome structure, the Dhyanalinga's energies allow even those unaware of meditation to experience a deep state of meditativeness, revealing the essential nature of life.

A special feature of the Dhyanalinga complex are the Teerthakunds, consecrated subterranean water bodies, energized by *rasalinga*s. A dip in these vibrant pools significantly enhances one's spiritual receptivity and is a good preparation to receive the Grace of the Dhyanalinga. The waters of the Teerthakunds also rejuvenate the body, and bring health and well-being.

The Dhyanalinga draws many thousands of people every week, who converge to experience a deep sense of inner peace.

Learn more at dhyanalinga.org.

LINGA BHAIRAVI

Adjacent to the Dhyanalinga, near the Isha Yoga Center, is the Linga Bhairavi. Consecrated by Sadhguru, Linga Bhairavi is an exuberant expression of the Divine Feminine – fierce and compassionate at once. Representing the creative and nurturing aspects of the universe, the Devi allows devotees to go through life effortlessly; all physical aspects of their lives – health, success, and prosperity – will find nourishment. A variety of rituals and offerings are available for one to connect with the Devi's outpouring Grace.

Learn more at lingabhairavi.org.

INNER ENGINEERING

Inner Engineering Online

Inner Engineering Online is a technology for well-being derived from the science of Yoga. Comprising of seven 90-minute sessions, it is offered as a comprehensive course for personal growth that brings about a shift in the way you perceive and experience your life, your work, and the world that you live in.

The objective of the program is to render you to explore your highest potential through powerful processes of self-transformation, distilled essence of classical Yoga, meditations to address key aspects of life and access to secrets of ancient wisdom.

Inner Engineering offers a unique opportunity for self-exploration and transformation, leading to a life of fulfillment and joy.

Inner Engineering Completion

After Inner Engineering Online, you can take your experience a step deeper with Inner Engineering Completion (also available as an online program). Designed by Sadhguru, the program offers the transmission of Shambhavi Mahamudra Kriya, a powerful and purifying 21-minute energy technique which incorporates the breath, along with rejuvenating and invigorating asanas.

Shambhavi Mahamudra Kriya aligns your entire system so that your body, mind, emotions and energies function in harmony, establishing a chemistry of blissfulness within you and empowering you to create your life the way you want it.

Today, millions of dedicated practitioners have experienced greater emotional balance, mental clarity, focus, stability, and improved health.

For more details, visit innerengineering.com.

ISHA KRIYA

Isha Kriya™ is a simple yet potent practice created by Sadhguru, which is drawn from the wisdom of Indian spirituality. The word *kriya* literally means "internal action", while "Isha" refers to that which is the source of creation. The purpose of Isha Kriya is to help an individual get in touch with the source of one's existence, in order to create life according to one's wish and vision.

Provided as a free guided meditation online and available with written instructions as well, Isha Kriya offers the possibility to experience the boundless energy within.

Daily practice of Isha Kriya brings health, dynamism, peace and well-being. It offers tools to cope with the hectic pace of modern life.

Learn more at ishakriya.com.